Artificial Intelligence
and Economic Analysis

Artificial Intelligence and Economic Analysis

Prospects and Problems

Edited by

Scott Moss

Faculty of Management and Business
Manchester Polytechnic

John Rae

Information Technology Institute
University of Salford

Edward Elgar

Published by
Edward Elgar Publishing Limited
Gower House
Croft Road
Aldershot
Hants GU11 3HR
England

Edward Elgar Publishing Company
Old Post Road
Brookfield
Vermont 05036
USA

A CIP catalogue record for this book
is available from the British Library.

Library of Congress Cataloging-in-Publication Data

Moss, Scott J.
    Artificial Intelligence and Economic Analysis: prospects and
    problems / Scott Moss, John Rae
    p. cm.

Includes bibliographical references and index.
1. Economics - Data processing. 2. Artificial intelligence.
I. Rae, John. II. Title.
HB 143.5.M67 1992   92-8913
330¹. 028563-dc20   CIP

ISBN 978 1 85278 685 4

Printed and bound by CPI Group (UK) Ltd, Croydon, CR0 4YY

Contents

List of Figures and Tables

Figures

Tables

List of Contributors

Luca Anderlini is Professor of Economics at St John's College, Cambridge.

Mike Artis is lecturer at the University of Manchester.

Huw Dixon is Professor of Economics at the University of York.

John D. Hey is Professor of Economics and Statistics, and Co-Director of the course for Experimental Economics at the University of York.

Robin Marris is Emeritus Professor at Birkbeck College, London.

Scott Moss is Senior Lecturer at Manchester Polytechnic.

Paul Ormerod is Economics Director at the Henley Centre for Forecasting.

John Rae is Lecturer at the Information Technology Institute at the University of Salford.

Martin Reynolds is Professor and Head of Department of Finance and Business Information Systems at Nottingham Polytechnic.

A. Romeo is Head of Economic Analysis at Unilever plc, London.

Paul Stoneman is Research Professor and Director of the Research Bureau at Warwick Business School, University of Warwick.

Acknowledgements

Funding for the conference which gave rise to this volume came from the HCI Initiative of the Medical Research Council, the Science and Engineering Research Council, the Economic and Social Research Council, HM Department of Trade and Industry and from the Manchester Polytechnic Faculty of Management and Business. We are especially grateful for the support and encouragement we had from Professor Andrew Lock. He guaranteed the finance for the conference at the outset (before external funding had been secured) and arranged for all non-academic administrative matters to be handled by his Faculty's Business Development Centre. Chris Bagley undertook the administration with the sort of professionalism and efficiency that makes it a pleasure for academics to organize these events. We would also like to thank Angela Cross who prepared the manuscript for publication.

1. Introduction

The Purpose of the Volume

With one exception, all of the papers in this volume are highly speculative. They were prepared for a conference held at Manchester Polytechnic in December 1990. The purpose of that conference, and hence this book, was to consider what, if anything, developments in the science of artificial intelligence (AI) could offer economists.

Why Artificial-Intelligence?

Artificial-intelligence is concerned with determining courses of action in problem spaces which are too large or complex for the application of constrained-optimization algorithms. Since all neoclassical economic models describe decision-making as a process of constrained optimization, it would appear that artificial-intelligence techniques offer the possibility of extending our representations of economic behaviour to take complexity into account.

It is useful in this regard to distinguish between two types of complexity which might affect economic models and modelling procedures. The first I will call environmental complexity and the second I will call outcome complexity.

We have environmental complexity when the set of information which could be obtained and the set of relationships among the various items of information are of sizes which are so large that they exceed the information-processing capacities of decision-makers. The game of chess provides an example of environmental complexity. Consider the following factoid: if the fastest existing super-computer were to calculate its optimal first move in a game of chess by considering all possible sets of moves from the opening to the endgame, then it would have to make that first move in the dark. For the sun would long since have burned out! Suppose, as in economic reality, the number of players is usually greater than two, and they do not have to abide by any clearly stated set of rules, then

1

we must abandon any suggestion that optimization over the problem space is tractable.

We have outcome complexity when simple models can yield a larger number of outcomes (usually time paths of variable values) than can be used to reach or predict either a single decision or a probability distribution of decisions. Models yielding either sunspot equilibria or deterministically chaotic outcomes are complex in this sense.

The development of economic analyses of outcome complexity is now reasonably well established. Although a number of papers on environmental complexity are circulating amongst interested scholars, their publication is only now getting underway.

This volume is intended as a contribution to the development of the analysis of environmental complexity. The purpose of this volume is to raise a number of issues about the analysis of environmental complexity; to compare AI-based approaches with conventional economists' approaches to particular subjects; to compare AI-based approaches which seem close to existing neoclassical approaches with some that do not; and to identify some areas in which those of us working in Britain are already making some progress.

The contributors to this volume were asked not simply to report established results, which are appropriately published in the refereed journals. Early results which are suggestive in that they open up rather than answer questions were solicited. So, too, were papers by established mainstream economists who were willing to express their own views about the limits of mainstream economic modelling and AI-based economic modelling. Virtually all of the contributors accommodated us in this regard.

Theory, Model and Modelling Technique

I do not intend here to enter into a philosophical or semantic discussion of the difference between a theory and a model. In this introduction, by theory I mean a set of statements which provide the criteria of what is analytically interesting and which specify appropriate representations of environmental and individual behaviour. A model is a set of relationships which can be manipulated to yield either quantitative or non-quantitative symbolic results. A modelling technique is a means of performing those manipulations. I suppose what I have called a theory might be a paradigm or a research programme to Kuhnians or Lakatosians. I believe that my use of the word 'model' is what every economist means by the word, and similarly with the phrase 'modelling technique'.

What we mean by neoclassical theory is clear. I don't think anyone would dispute Lionel Robbins'(1935) statement that it is a theory of resource allocation in conditions of scarcity. The allocation of resources is usually by individuals. The scarcities are represented by constraints and the allocation reflects individual preferences represented by an objective function. In other words, the appropriate representation of individual behaviour is always a constrained-optimization set-up. The environment is always represented as a set of constraints. The appropriate modelling techniques are either algorithms for solving constrained optimization problems or methods (usually based on fixed-point theorems) for proving that particular constrained-optimization set-ups have solutions.

Does economics have to be about the allocation of resources in conditions of scarcity? I suspect that that is an issue which will always be a part of economics - but perhaps not the whole of it. Consider the Stiglerian theory of search which underlies all neoclassical models involving the acquisition of information. In these models, there is a probability distribution of outcomes and a cost of sampling that distribution. The probability distribution is fully specified and there is no physical limit to how much of the distribution can be sampled. That distribution is the set of available information. The information-processing capacity of decision-makers is sufficient to sample every element in that information set. They do not sample every element because, though to do so would be feasible, it would also be uneconomic. However, the information-processing capacity of decision-makers is by no means scarce.

Another way of looking at this issue is in relation to computational capacity. Radner (1966) proved some 25 years ago that unlimited computational capacity on the part of each agent is a necessary condition for the existence of a general equilibrium. A more recent literature, reviewed in this volume by Anderlini, is based on the reasonable presumption that in either single or repeated economic games, rationality must be bounded unless the solutions to economic problems facing agents can, in principle, be computed. This is, of course, stronger than requiring the existence of a solution. However, as Anderlini points out, the question is not whether in practice agents have the computational capacity to compute a solution but, rather, whether some computational capacity would be sufficient to compute a solution.

The issues involved here are by no means trivial. There are economic allocation problems which cannot be solved, either because the solution is not computable in principle; because limited computational capacity prevents its solution even if it is computable; or because limited information-processing capacities render impracticable the specification of the constraints and possibly the objective functions.

One possibility stemming from these results is that there are problems to which traditional methods of economic analysis are applicable and problems to which they are not. Unfortunately, the criteria of applicability are not easy to specify. For example, a plausible set of criteria of applicability are the existence and the computability of constrained-optimization solutions together with sufficient information-processing (or computational) capacity on the part of decision-makers actually to compute the solutions. Such criteria imply that economic analysis is synonymous with operational research, or perhaps decision theory. However, as Stoneman (Chapter 7) argues, economic analysis is concerned with both a higher level of aggregation and a higher level of abstraction than operational research. The real question for him is whether the application of AI or other simulation techniques yield results which are different from results obtained with traditional techniques. If the results are much the same, then artificially intelligent agents are acting as if they were constrained optimizers. The implication here is that such results strengthen the case for using neoclassical methods.

Dixon (Chapter 8) bases his argument on the absence of any model of reasoning in neoclassical economic analysis. He believes that the proponents of AI applications to economic analysis have 'to demonstrate that there is both a clear need and a payoff' to the modelling of reasoning. There are areas of economics where such a payoff is likely. Dixon mentions specifically the modelling of disequilibrium processes and the modelling of the choice of strategies in game theoretic settings.

What about cases where the results are different or where results are simply unattainable by means of traditional analytical techniques? (There are no cases where conventional algorithms can and AI techniques cannot find a constrained optimum.) Stoneman, in discussion, asserts that all problems can be specified as constrained-optimization problems and complexity can be assumed away. If this is true, then we are only left with cases where, for the same problem space and information space, AI-based techniques yield results which are different from results obtained by conventional techniques. This will happen only where the problem and information spaces are so large that conventional analysis requires simplifying assumptions. It seems likely that, in such cases, neither kind of analytical technique can be expected with certainty to find a global optimum - if one exists.

One line of research suggested by these remarks is an investigation of the effects of simplifying assumptions vis-à-vis rules of thumb - both in relation to optimal results. Romeo and Moss (Chapter 5) argue that via the use of expert system-type rules, the nature of oligopolistic behaviour can be explored and the results are both rich and practically useful.

In general, we can say that economic theory based on techniques of artificial intelligence will be concerned with decision-making in environments where the information available exceeds the information-processing capacities of decision-makers. It may be that, in principle, no amount of information-processing capacity will be sufficient to determine optimal decisions, or simply that the information-processing resources required are unavailable or too expensive to be economic. AI techniques then provide a means of modelling search over such large information sets, of modelling learning behaviour and of relating perceived environmental conditions to actions.

The Contributions to this Volume

Everyone who is engaged in the modelling of learning behaviour and decision-making - whether committed neoclassicals or not - use condition-action pairs to represent behaviour. A condition-action pair is a 2-tuple in which one element specifies aspects of the current state of the environment, and the other element specifies a set of actions. Particular representations of these condition-action pairs vary considerably. In some models, each element is a string drawn from a trinary alphabet. In others, rules of the sort familiar from expert systems are used. Learning can be represented as a process of selection from a population of possible rules changing by a process of random variation or by some more systematic means. The more systematic means can rely on expert system-type rules for modifying rules of action, or they can use non-linear updating equations to link conditions and actions. Which of these techniques is used depends on the purpose of the models.

Marris (Chapter 2) believes strongly that we must represent decision-making in the most realistic possible way. Presently, parallel distributed systems (PDSs) are thought to provide the best replication of human cognition. For this reason, Marris argues that individuals are best represented as PDSs.

Moss (Chapter 3) takes a different view. His work is not intended to replicate human cognition but is instead intended to analyse, and where possible, improve decision-making processes in economic systems. The relevant questions for Moss include: 'At which locations in the system should different kinds of decision be taken?'; 'Which sources of information should be used?'; 'How can the onset of failure be recognized at an early stage?'; 'How are unforeseen opportunities to be recognized in time to take advantage of them?'. Answering these questions requires a representation of the system's environment by means of equations, inequalities, and perhaps rules expressing non-quantitative relationships. Apart from the non-quantitative relationships, the representation of the environment entails traditional economic modelling techniques.

Though Marris is by no means concerned to support conventional, neoclassical analysis, his concern correctly to model cognition has previously been shared by conventionally mainstream economists.[1] PDSs, genetic algorithms, least-squares learning and moving-average learning schemes differ from the sort of rule-based learning schemes favoured by Moss or by Rae and Reynolds (Chapter 4), Hey and Reynolds (Chapter 6) and Artis, Moss and Ormerod (Chapter 10) in that they yield results without any practicable means of ascribing detailed reasons for those results. Moss demonstrates in Chapter 3 the sorts of detailed explanations which are possible using rule-based models, and discusses the difficulty of obtaining the same detail of explanation using the other modelling techniques. Such explanations are important if economic process is the subject of analysis. They are less important if the only interest is in the attainment of equilibrium.

Different sources of representations of individual behaviour are described in the papers by Rae and Reynolds, Hey and Reynolds and Artis, Moss and Ormerod.

Rae and Reynolds report an adaptive learning mechanism which is tested and proved in the context of a monopoly model. Their substantive concern is with the process of economic decision-making rather than with equilibrium outcomes. Since the completion of the first version of the paper included in this volume, other papers have appeared reporting results with adaptive learning mechanisms in otherwise conventional neoclassical models. However, the insistence by Rae and Reynolds of the importance of analysing economic processes, and the lack of relevance of equilibrium results in this regard, remains important. The paper is also distinguished from the other literature on adaptive learning in economic models in that convergence to a rational-expectations or Nash equilibrium is not taken to be a matter of any moment.

The Hey and Reynolds paper and the Artis, Moss and Ormerod paper take two quite different approaches to the formalization of actual decision-making processes.

Hey and Reynolds set up an experiment to test the patent-race models

---

[1] cf. Marimon, McGrattan and Sargent (1989) and Arifovic (1990).

found in the industrial economics literature. In that literature, published models usually entail a Nash equilibrium outcome. In addition to investigating whether the theoretical result is realized in controlled experiments, Hey and Reynolds formalize the decision-making processes of the subjects in the experiments. This formalization, as they show, can lead to the specification of rules describing subjects' behaviour - whether or not this behaviour leads to equilibrium outcomes.

Artis, Moss and Ormerod argue that models of learning and decision-making behaviour developed in relation to analyses of competitive strategies can also be applied to economic forecasting. These techniques allow for the inclusion of expert judgement in forecasting models in a way which yields not only improved forecasts, but also detailed explanations of the judgements which influence the forecasts.

Implications for Continuing Research

In this volume, Anderlini, Dixon and Stoneman have put the view that techniques from the science of artificial intelligence can, and perhaps should, be used within a fundamentally neoclassical framework. On the other side, the papers by Rae and Reynolds and by Hey and Reynolds use and/or suggest applications of AI techniques to demonstrate the limits of neoclassical analysis. Marris and Moss suggest quite different techniques for extending our understanding of economic behaviour without limiting that understanding by working within any particular economic analytical tradition. In quite a different vein, Artis, Moss and Ormerod seek to use AI techniques to formalize some aspects of economic analysis which are presently left to informal judgements by analysts.

These contributions cover the range of applications of AI known to us to be currently under development in Britain. That range of interests is distinctive. Unlike the American work represented by, for example, the working papers of the Santa Fe Institute Economics Research Program, developments in the UK are not seen as extensions of neoclassical economics. Most of us see no reason to be bound by the limits of what is interesting in the light of neoclassical theory. This view is shared by the Trento group of Italian economists interested in applications of artificial intelligence. Papers emanating from the Trento group (e.g. Warglein (1991)) generate examples of machine learning which they believe to be applicable to economic analysis. The economic applications have not yet been developed as they have in Britain.

For the present, I suspect that we will continue to see the development of three quite distinct lines of AI-oriented research in economics: applications intended to extend neoclassical theory, applications intended to undermine neoclassical theory, and applications which ignore neoclassical theory in the quest for new modelling techniques and fields of analysis. Because we are in the earliest stages of the development of AI approaches to economics, it is obviously right that such a broad range of applications should be developed. As Charniak and McDermott (1985) wrote in the wake of the hugely expensive and minimally productive research into machine translation: 'That simple ideas do not necessarily scale up to real-world problems is a lesson we in artificial-intelligence have been taught many times. The trick is to remember the lesson each time before investing too heavily in a particular bag of ideas.'

A wide-ranging set of approaches with discussion and open-minded exchanges of ideas and results seem most likely to ensure that economists' collective investment in this particular bag of ideas will be efficient. Certainly, the conference which gave rise to the present volume was characterized by good humour and open-mindedness.

2. Economics and Intelligence

Robin Marris

The Nature of 'Intelligence'

In order to discuss the subject of economics and artificial intelligence, it is just as important to think first about the meaning of the main word as its qualifier; otherwise there is a tendency for some confusion concerning what it is we are trying to imitate. 'Intelligence' originally described a capacity in the mental performance of higher animals, including humans; thus we refer to 'intelligent beings'. Basically, the word refers to 'high' levels in the performance of nervous systems - the capacity for extremely sophisticated learning-based decision-taking. All kinds of lower animals, worms, amoebas, viruses, and mechanical widgets can take simple decisions but, or at least we like to suppose, worms cannot have complex thoughts or take complex decisions, like maximizing utility or discounting cash flow. In short, intelligence is a property of advanced brains. Unfortunately, although there has been quite an amount of laboratory observation on monkey brains, for familiar reasons there is very little similar research material on human brains. Despite this, the whole of economics is based on quite complex implicit axioms concerning the working of the brain: if I assume that Economic Man is a utility-maximizing mechanism, I am implicitly assuming his brain is one kind of biological machine rather than another. The traditional proposition that I am merely arguing 'as if' it was a maximizing mechanism, and therefore need not worry about what it actually is, does not stand up. More precisely, it does not stand up if we wish to continue to regard economics as a science.

Enter the Brain

We know the brain is a remarkable machine. It can organize conferences. It can do higher mathematics. It can compose music. It can sail boats (and once it has learned to sail, or to swim, to walk,

11

to bicycle, to ski, to drive a car or fly a plane; it puts the knowledge into deep store, never forgets it, and recalls it for use without apparent conscious reprocessing).

But, in the 'AI' context, there is still more. Clearly the brain works without a program, or alternatively is, especially at the highest levels, self-programming (e.g. it makes mental models, e.g. it teaches itself to ski). It can use data that are inaccurate or incomplete. It can make spontaneous generalizations. It can make inductions. It can find information without knowing precisely what it is looking for - 'content-addressing' the memory. It records its own activities and records the recording of them. It spontaneously creates internal mental models and at will stores, accesses and develops these. It can transfer mental models from one domain to another, and is thus, unlike the great majority of 'artificially intelligent' machines, at least until recently, able to make decisions in unfamiliar situations.

In addition to all this 'fuzzy' activity, we know the brain is not a bad performer in unfuzzy logic and also, in the past half century, has achieved the remarkable feat of creating an artifact, the computer, to powerfully enhance its own logical capacities, or, more precisely, an artificial aid to offset its patent weakness (as a logical machine) in respect of calculation speed and short-term storage capacity.

The Role of Evolution

Up to that point, the brain had developed largely by biological evolution, implying that its intelligence capacity was substantially completed maybe half a million years ago. At some point there biologically evolved in man the capacity for rich language, which the highest apes, it now seems, physically do not possess. But the extremely recent developments of the capacity for writing, printing and now computing, are the result of cultural evolution, i.e. they are passed on, by means of their very own communicating powers, from one generation to the next.

Nevertheless, the fact that the brain originally evolved by a Darwinian process is extremely relevant to everything we think and say about it. Evolution is a powerful, but untidy, form of search.

A MESSAGE FROM BRAIN SCIENCE

Francis Crick, Nobel Laureate, FRS, following his historic contributions to molecular biology and genetics, which began with the discovery of the helical structure of DNA in the 1950's, has for the past decade and a half devoted himself to the study of the brain, and has published a number of papers in the field: the paper cited in the references (Towards a Neurobiological theory of Consciousness (Crick and Kock, 1990)) appears to the present author to have the potentiality of a break-through almost on the scale of the famous helix. A Fellow of the Salk Institute, he resides in San Diego and was a member of the working group which led to the publication of Rummelhart et al, the 'PDP' book discussed in the adjoining text. Recently, he wrote a lucid account of the topic in the international science journal, *Nature* ('The recent excitement about neural networks', 12 Jan. 1989). This contains a rather choice passage, aimed primarily at psychologists, but which also aptly applies, with little modification, to economists, to organization theorists, and to other cognitive and social scientists.

'It comes as a surprise to neuroscientists to discover that many psychologists, linguists in particular, have very little or no interest in the actual brain, or at least what goes on inside it. The brain, they feel, is far too complicated to understand. Far better to produce simple models which do the job in an intelligible manner. That such models have little resemblance to the way the brain actually behaves is not seen as a serious criticism. It if describes, in a succinct way, some of the psychological data, what can be wrong with that? Notice, however, that by using such arguments, one could easily make a good case for alchemy or for the existence of phlogiston. ...I suspect that within most modellers a frustrated mathematician is trying to unfold his wings. It is not enough to make something that works. How much better if it can be shown to embody some powerful general principle for handling information, expressible in deep mathematical form, if only to give an air of respectability to an otherwise rather lowbrow enterprise.'

Only the dimmest economist will fail to recognize how few words would need to be substituted to make this appear like a quotation from our methodological controversies. Is it proper for us to take no interest in the actual nature of that thing (namely human intelligence) which, by the application of the word 'intelligent' we avow we are trying to mimic?

ANOTHER MESSAGE FROM BRAIN SCIENCE

In the Crick and Kock (1990, see above) paper, which is discussed below, we find another pertinent quotation, whose general force will be apparent to many AI readers and will become further so below.

'The most effective way to approach the problem of consciousness would be to use the descriptions of psychologists and cognitive scientists and attempt to map different aspects of their models onto what is known about the neuroanatomy and neurophysiology of the brain. Naturally, we have attempted to do this, but we have not found it as useful as one might hope, though such models do point to the importance of attention and short-term memory and suggest that consciousness should have easy access to the higher, planning levels of the system. *A major handicap is the pernicious influence of the paradigm of the Von Neuman serial computer.* It is a painful business to try to translate the various boxes labelled 'files', 'CPU', 'buffer' etc. occurring in psychological models, each with its own special methods of processing, into the language of neuronal activity and interaction. This is mainly because present-day computers make use of precisely-detailed pulse-coded messages. There is no convincing evidence that the brain uses such a system, and much to suggest that it does not.' [Italics added.]

Consequently, it is absolutely certain that the architecture of the brain is not something that would result from comprehensive design. It follows that if we build models assuming that the structure of the brain, or of organizations (which are networks of brains) is efficient or 'rational', however interesting the models may be, since they do not tell us how individual humans function, they could not tell us how organizations function. For example, it is widely believed by modern geneticists that the brain evolved to meet the challenge of sight and movement. Organisms that could do complex movements and eventually could 'see' had superior fitness for survival. This could suggest that the capacity to learn complex procedures, such as skiing, (not the procedure itself, of course) is a form of inherited

ROM. That might explain the extraordinary phenomenon, already mentioned, that just as we inherit the unconscious capacity to blink our eye with enormous speed in face of small flying objects, so, after being learned, capacities such as driving, cycling, sailing or skiing seem to pass into the unconscious.

The 'Biological Challenge' to AI

It is the general practice of people working in the field of AI, whether they are specifically concerned with organizations or not, that they take for granted that the scarcity of direct observation on the actual brain is so great that it is virtually a waste of time to think about it at all. Instead, what has been described as a 'functional' approach is adopted, i.e. we develop models which may appear to imitate an intelligent function, but not the biological brain's physical method of carrying out that function: we try to imitate nature, without necessarily following her. To some extent, given the experimental situation, this is inevitable. Either we do it that way or we seek other employment.

It is not the purpose of the present paper to cause an increase in academic unemployment by insisting that until a date, maybe many years hence, when a realistic comprehensive biological model of the human brain has appeared, all research should cease. Rather I wish to point to some intellectual dangers involved in the social scientists's in general, and the economists's in particular, present typical approach, especially at the conceptual end of the field. At minimum I wish to plead that we should always ask the question, 'Is the model I am contemplating building a plausible analogy to the way the corresponding function might be conducted by the biological brain?'. Let us call this question the 'biological challenge'.

It could be that the 'intelligent' function or activity we have modelled is not, in fact, a function of the brain, but rather is something different (surely this is the case with classic expert systems?). Of course, it may well be that despite the negative conclusion, my model is nevertheless going to do something that is in some other way useful to the human race or to its organizations. Such a development has occurred recently in the case of PDP, where the concept, while advancing, but by no means revolutionizing, our understanding of the biological brain, has found immediate, spectacularly successful applications in search-oriented computing.

Nevertheless, as I hope to show by a scheme of propositions (see below), there are strong reasons why economists should always face up to the biological challenge, if only to look for possibly unexpected aspects of their programme. Researchers should arm themselves with at least a minimum familiarity with a selection from the biological literature, such as found in the references to the present paper.

Neural Nets

What is the most general definition of a neural net? Let us say that it consists of a set of entities, for the sake of argument called 'neurons', that have the property that in response to inputs they produce outputs that are some non-linear function of the inputs; the plurals indicate the possibility of multiple inputs and outputs; the neuron may range in complexity from that of the simplest of logic gates to that of a micro processor.

A net consists of a layered set of neurons where every neuron in one layer is connected to every member of another layer: the two-layer net is a limiting case. The strength of connections, however, varies on the different pathways. The input received by one neuron in consequence of the output from another, depends on both the original strength of the output and the connection strength of the pathway from the one neuron to the other. Thus inputs, outputs and connection strengths may be seen as numbers, and the effective input from neuron A to neuron B is the product of the output of A (which is the same in all directions, like a lighthouse signal), multiplied by the connection strength or weight of B from A. The connection strengths are not inherently constant, but rather may change through real time, i.e. may be *learned*.

Layerings may be partly circular, i.e. in a three-layer system, all neurons in the first layer are potentially connected with all in the second, and all in the second with all in the third; but the third layer, perhaps, may be connected to the first. In addition there may be exogenous inputs to individual neurons, and it may be possible to read the outputs.

With given weights, if input stimulus is applied, activity will spread through the system, and may eventually stabilize, permanently or transiently. The resulting set of steady-state 'firings' (meaning that the pattern of firings is repeating rather than developing) can be described as the 'settling' of the net, or 'output' of the input. Evidently, the relationship between output and input will be essentially determined, in a complex way, by the connection strengths. It follows that nets can be taught to associate outputs with inputs. They can in fact be taught numerous pairs of associations. Thus a single set of numbers, namely the connection strengths, can represent numerous associations.

But because the associations may be overlapping, the net has two crucial brain-like properties, namely, (a) when given a correct input it may produce the wrong output, and (b) when given an incorrect or incomplete input it will give an output which may be the correct output, and is more likely to be so the less the inaccuracy or incompleteness of the input.

The connection strengths, not the neurons, contain the 'memory' or 'database' of the system. It is content-addressable. In order to define what this memory 'knows' concerning a particular association, one must consider all the connection strengths. (Of course, in order to see what it knows, we must also fire the neurons.) If a connection strength is conceived as a piece of information, then every piece relates to every data item; it is the collectivity that makes the information. This is called a distributed system. So we have parallel distributed processing, or PDP. As most people will know, there has been excited speculation that this is the kind of way a brain might work. The mass of 'white matter', i.e. connections, in a real-life brain is certainly much heavier than that of 'grey matter', i.e. the neurons.

In reality, major qualifications are already known, of which three are especially relevant:

a.   The relevant part of the brain, i.e. that which stores long-term memory, the neocortex, could not be one big net; it would be far too big and therefore far too slow; consequently, if the brain is neural-net-like, it must be a net of nets: alternatively or additionally it is a net arranged in modules (see Rummelhart et al., 1988, chapter 17).

b.   The methods of 'training' adopted in the simulation models are most unlikely to be used by the actual brain.

c.   Neural nets will not do logic, nor probably take decisions; there must be some other form of short-term memory and processing for this (however, we cannot see any evidence for such a thing physically, this function seems likely itself to be distributed through the brain anatomy, possibly as a mode of using neurons). But there is a definite biological reason for major limitations on this short-term memory and processing capacity (see Crick and Kock, 1990).

Consciousness

Although social scientists do not generally appreciate this, the phenomenon of consciousness is crucial to all normative aspects of our disciplines and to many positive aspects. It is certainly crucial to the concept of rationality and hence to that of bounded rationality. Rationality means behaving according to a well-specified and comprehensive set of preferences. 'Bounded' rationality means doing the same, subject to constraint on the amount of information (out of all the potentially relevant information) which can in practice be processed in the course of attempting to make these decisions.

Horrible Thoughts

Suppose that the experiences and associations stored in the long-term distributed memory are what, after formation into categories, inform our preferences. If those preferences are then processed by the limited short-term memory and processor for the purpose of conversion into decisions, various horrible questions jump out:

a.   Can we expect the resulting decisions to be consistent? Most brain scientists will answer a resounding negative. What happens then to the axiomatic base of social choice theory?

b. Given the vast capacity of this memory, why should not its capacity be regarded as unbounded?

c. If the boundary problem is considered to be located in the limited short-term processing capacity, are we really saying that the decisions of humans and organizations can be informed by no more than the amount of information that can be held in the short-term stack? This being a reductio ad absurdum, the whole concept of bounded rationality could thus seem to have run into a contradiction.

These 'pensées horribles' suggest that a position on the nature of consciousness and of its relation to the various kinds of memory, is essential to all our studies.

Crick and Kock

In the forthcoming paper (Crick and Kock, 1990), the authors emphasize the close connection between understanding the nature of consciousness and identifying different types of animal and human memory. They distinguish:

1. Types of memory
    a. Iconic   accurate and detailed, but short-lived e.g. 1/10th sec.

    b. Short term   seconds, minutes, limited storage, e.g. equivalent of seven digits.

    c. Procedural   procedures for skiing, swimming etc.

    d. Long term   probably a net of neural nets; huge capacity and other properties etc as discussed above; let us ('we' = present

author, not Crick and Kock) tentatively
call it a 'supernet'.

In the view of Crick and Kock, consciousness involves attention,
awareness and short-term memory. The other forms of memory are
not essentially involved with consciousness. Evidently, when
conscious, we take information out of long-term memory and do
logical operations on it. Evidently, the way data are kept in long-term
memory is something much more complex and sophisticated than the
way described in an elementary account, such as above, of a neural
net. There must be hierarchies of categorizations, generalizations,
abstractions, mental models and so forth.

2. The operating system

How, in the condition we may timidly call consciousness, does the
short-term processor interact with the long-term one? In the crudest
practical terms, how does a basically restricted system draw data
from a supernet, given that the data involved in any one subject are
liable to be distributed all over it? Crick and Kock suggest that the
answer may be 'binding', that is, some way of putting in a special
cross-net linkage between the involved neurons. But in the nature of
things it seems unlikely that this could be effectively done with
white-matter links, especially as great speed is required. Crick and
Kock's dramatic suggestion is that it may be done by synchronized
firing patterns, and, indeed, it does seem that correlated firing,
creating a wave-form, around 30-50 Herz, has been observed in
lightly anaesthetized monkeys, in neurons which can be proved to be
associated with specific external stimuli.

In short, Crick and Kock are suggesting that consciousness is an
operating mode of the brain that has, or will be found to have, a
specific electrochemical description. This is not inconsistent with the
suggestion of Rummelhart and McClelland (1989, chapter 14) that
the content of consciousness is sequential settling, on a time-scale of
microseconds, of a net. If this model is gradually validated, it will
undoubtedly have a major effect on our whole way of thinking about
how we think. That is to say, if we wish to postulate that, e.g.,

inductive thinking can be described by a certain type of cognitive model (e.g. classifiers), we shall need to test the idea against an increasingly definite physical model of what the brain, when conscious, actually does. Furthermore, we shall increasingly be forced to face up to the question of whether this or that type of operation which we are proposing to model, is supposed to occur in this or that type of memory.

Stylized Conclusions

A.   The human brain is a neural supernet.
B.   Organizations are networks of human brains.
C.   Economic systems are networks of organizations.
D.   Features of the brain:

1.   The deep memory
    a.   distributed in a net of nets
    b.   access is associatively content-addressable
    c.   inaccurate
    d.   but able to work with incomplete or inaccurate instructions
    e.   total capacity is so large as to be quasi-infinite; i.e. this (unconscious) memory is quasi-unbounded
    f.   the brain as a whole either inherits or develops a more sequential mode for logical operations and 'thinking' generally
    g.   when this mode is active, we are conscious, then
        (1)   the short-term memory does logical work
        (2)   it interacts continuously with the deep memory

2.   The IOS (Input-Output System) of the brain
    a.   eyes, ears, miscellaneous 'senses'
    b.   coded into 'language'
    c.   processing capacity
        (1)   orders of magnitude smaller than internal capacity (the IOS is a bottleneck)
        (2)   employs some parallel and analogue modes

3.   Features of the short-term processor
        a.   severely limited
        b.   access content-addressable yet accurate
        c.   consequently 'mental arithmetic' and general logical
        ability is effective but highly constrained, i.e. bounded

4.   Learning
        a.   means changing the deep memory, especially the
                mental models stored therein; some, but not all,
                learning processes pass through the short-term
                memory

5.   Rationality
        a.   preferences are partly ROM (only the most primitive)
                mostly learned
        b.   they must mainly reside in deep memory
        c.   they are activated by consciousness
        d.   rationality means behaving in accordance with
                preferences
        e.   bounded rationality is caused by the poor processing
                capacity of the conscious
        f.   if, as may be the case, the brain has methods of
                converging to consistency with deep preferences,
                bounded rationality may be less significant than
                usually assumed
        g.   but the total picture casts doubt on the whole concept
                of rationality, since in this type of system there is no
                internal requirement for consistent behaviour, and no
                external method (owing to the boundedness) of
                imposing it.

Expectations

The human brain has the capacity to make some kind of decision in
face of apparently unique situations. It is therefore able to 'live with'
the need to make forecasts concerning events for which there are no
data for statistical estimates (Knightian uncertainty). Thus Keynes

(Treatise on Probability, 1921) argued that we must be able to form subjective probabilities concerning future developments for which there are no statistical past experience. This was the whole basis of his attack of classical probability theory, and also on econometrics. We all agree up to a point, that is we know that 'rational' or 'consistent' expectational models, based on systematic, statistical learning, are vulnerable to the Keynesian critique, but there the controversy stops. How does the brain do this particular thing that we know computers cannot do that is, take decisions on apparently no information? The usual answer is 'intuition', but what can this possibly mean?

The answer has to be that in every decision the brain applies not a limited, accurate, specific, 'local' database, already determined to be relevant to the problem in hand, but rather, to a degree, the whole of its memory. How is that physically possible? Answer, by means of a net of nets. By this means it can, for example, find analogies in apparently remote fields. It can also use qualitative and analytical information. We all have a good idea how to conduct our lives in face of the finite probability that tomorrow a nuclear bomb will explode, but if you ask a group of people to give numerical probabilities for this, they will answer in the range of from one in three to one in a million. Furthermore, the answers will prove to be correlated with political opinions.

Macroeconomic expectations at any moment are the product of a social net of human-brain supernets, the communications between brains being much more constrained than the communication within brains. Given the necessary fragility of the expectations of an individual, the expectations of the mass are liable to be subject to epidemics. Hence, without any obvious statistical basis, business optimism may change sharply from simply the result of one or two events. And typically these will be events which have no well-defined previous parallels.

3. Artificial-Intelligence Models of Complex Economic Systems

Scott Moss[1]

Introduction

A complex economic system is one in which the information-processing capacities of agents are limited relative to the information available to them. In practice, this means that agents are unable to identify (or at least to know whether they have identified) all of the constraints on their actions or, indeed, all of the arguments and parameters of their objective functions or functionals.

The common characteristic of artificial-intelligence techniques is that they solve problems in complex environments. For this reason, the science of artificial intelligence is a natural source of inspiration in developing the means of modelling economic decision-making behaviour in environments where complexity is a serious issue. The particular techniques to be used and how they are developed for purposes of economic modelling will reasonably depend on the objectives of the modeller. So what are these objectives?

One group of modellers, associated with the Santa Fe Institute, appear to see applications of artificial intelligence as natural extensions of prevailing orthodox economics. A typical question of concern to them is whether the results of rational expectations models are replicated in models where agents do not know the correct model of the economy and are unable to obtain full information about the

[1] In developing the approach described in this paper I have benefited greatly from discussions with my colleagues Michael Artis of the University of Manchester and Andrew Lock of Manchester Polytechnic. Financial support from the Nuffield Foundation, the Economic and Social Research Council and British Nuclear Fuels PLC is gratefully acknowledged. The responsibility for any errors of analysis or judgement rests entirely with me. The views expressed herein are those of the author.

current state of the world. In such models, agents are represented by machine-learning algorithms.[2]

Other modellers, including the author, are concerned with the process of making decisions in complex economic environments. The object of the modelling is to assess the power of various decision-making procedures. This object obviously owes more to the behavioural and evolutionary schools of economics than to the neoclassical school.

In the past, the neoclassical objective of relating actions to outcomes and the behaviouralists' objective of analysing economic processes did not overlap very much. Once economists turn their attention to complex economic systems and seek to adapt techniques from the science of artificial intelligence to analyse such systems, the overlap can become virtually complete to the benefit of both schools of thought.

The purpose of this paper is to explain why the overlap is both natural and fruitful.

The Purposes of Modelling in Complex Environments

In an environment where information-processing capacities are too limited to enable agents to assess all possible constraints, outcomes and their likelihoods, prediction by agents is not a viable goal. After all, how can one predict events which one cannot describe in advance? A corollary of this question relates to optimizing behaviour. Even if an agent's targets are clearly[3] comprehensible by him, and he recognizes a small and easily manipulated set of

---

[2]   The standard references here are Knight (1921), Radner (e.g. 1968) and Nelson and Winter (1982). See also Moss (1981, 1984).

[3]   A machine-learning algorithm is a procedure by means of which a computer program acquires and processes information in order to improve its performance in some well-defined way. Virtually all machine-learning algorithms entail the automated evaluation and modification of rules. The rules are all condition-action pairs: in states of nature satisfying a given set of conditions, the program initiates a given set of actions.

instruments, he cannot know the effects of his instruments on his targets because he cannot predict which state of nature will prevail at any date. This is because he cannot comprehend the range of possible states of nature.

The way round this difficulty has traditionally been to assert that there is some evolutionary process which ensures that those firms whose behaviour comes closest to optimizing behaviour will survive. In its most recent form, Marimon, McGrattan and Sargent (1989) have shown that rule-based behaviour by agents can evolve so as to bring about results compatible with those of rational-expectations macroeconomic models. This approach itself seems to bring neoclassical economics a long way towards behavioural economics, with its decision rules (or rules of thumb). What is involved here is the use of machine-learning techniques to model economic behaviour.

As we shall see below, machine learning can be used to model economic behaviour without telling us anything about the behavioural process - how agents do or should go about making decisions. Other machine-learning techniques shift our attention from action and outcome to the decision-making process. The latter techniques do not involve prior specification of mappings of states of nature into actions. Instead, they require, and sometimes develop, specifications of the ways in which agents learn to cope with mappings that do not perform well, and how they reinforce mappings that do generate successful performance. In effect, these techniques shift the focus of our attention from the effects of particular strategies to learning behaviour. Models are then[4] used to assess the effectiveness and efficiency of various approaches to learning - whether learning by doing, learning by using or learning from experts and 'the literature'.

Specifications of learning behaviour can be either descriptive or prescriptive. Descriptive specifications of learning behaviour can be treated as specifications of some aspects of the environment. For

---

[4]   It is important to note that one of the pre-eminent founders of the science of artificial intelligence and, in particular, machine-learning, was Herbert Simon - the founder of the school of behavioural economics.

example, in assessing possible marketing strategies, managers might do well to work with a specification of consumers' learning behaviour which they believe to be descriptively accurate, and to try different specifications of their own strategic responses to episodes of various kinds. The purpose would be to prescribe decision-making procedures for the marketing managers, and not to predict actual consumer behaviour or, consequently, their own actions in a competitive environment.

There already exists a viable technique for the analysis of decision-making procedures. This is the building of scenarios.[5] The basic idea is to trace out possible developments and to consider the results of different strategies for reacting to unforeseen outcomes. Decision-makers are enjoined from attaching any particular credibility to the scenarios and, even more importantly, from attaching probabilities of occurrence to the outcomes they consider. This seems an appropriate format for the analysis of decision-making and learning procedures. The point is to develop effective and flexible ways of responding to unforeseen events.

Whether machine-learning techniques can be used to automate the development and assessment of such scenarios is the subject of current research[6] In order to gain insights into decision-making from such scenario-building, the output available to program users must include the fullest possible explanations of simulated behaviour and outcomes. We shall see below how such explanations can be provided. Of course, simulation models which are intended only to demonstrate that the results of existing, equilibrium theories can be extended to complex environments, need not yield economically meaningful explanations. Only the results from simulation experiments are needed in order to make careful comparisons of those results and the predictions of neoclassical economic theory.

---

[5]   Brian Loasby (e.g. 1990) has discussed scenarios in relation to economic analysis.

[6] See Moss (1989).

The Techniques which are Presently Available

In this section, I describe two AI algorithms which have been developed or applied to an economic setting. One of these techniques has been used to extend existing economic theory to complex environments. The other is being developed to automate the building scenarios for managers.

The techniques with which we are concerned in general involve specifications of learning behaviour by simulated agents. Since the behaviour of these agents is determined by computer programs, any learning by them is, in effect, learning by the programs - that is, machine learning.

Most machine-learning programs proceed by induction. The general idea is that a program is presented with a series of 'learning examples', so that it can learn to discriminate among instances. The two main procedures in inductive machine learning are generalization and specialization. Both involve hierarchies of concepts.

Generalization involves some reduction in the number of conditions which place an object in a category. Specialization involves the creation of a new category in which objects satisfy a larger number of conditions. A hierarchy of categories with the conditions distinguishing the categories is, for these purposes, a model. In fact, it is not hard to represent the sort of mathematical models which dominate economics as hierarchical models.[7]

As far as I can see, the appropriate machine-learning techniques to use for economic analysis are inductive rather than deductive. The importance of experience in improving performance has been well accepted since Arrow's (1964) analysis of learning by doing. There was also Penrose's (1959) analysis of subjective knowledge which can be learned but not taught and is acquired only by engaging in activities. Later on, Rosenberg (1982) was inspired by his historical studies to define the related phenomenon of learning by using.

All of these specifications involve the notion that experience consists of incremental improvements in understandings of the relationship between action and outcome. As the conditions in which

---

[7]   See Goldberg (1989) for a detailed account of Holland's developments and a complete bibliography.

a given set of actions are followed by a desired outcome come to be better recognized, they also come to be a part of the decision-maker's routine. Routinization is a consequence of learning by induction. Condition-action pairs which are systematically followed by[8] desirable outcomes will come increasingly to be relied on without prior consideration or evaluation of alternatives. It is easy to represent this sort of inductive learning by formal algorithms.

Such routines can be generalized. For example, decision-makers could look for several condition-action pairs which have non-empty intersections of conditions and actions. That is, some conditions and some actions will be common to two or more successful condition-action pairs. It could then be worth considering whether the common elements of the condition-action pairs themselves yield successful condition-action pairs. We would then have a decision rule which applied to a larger number of states than either of the condition-action pairs. This is unambiguously a generalization which simplifies the record of the decision-maker's experience and speeds up decision-making.

Routines can also be specialized. The simplest specialization is to keep a record of the constituent condition-action pairs from which a generalization was formed and, if the generalization is not itself successful, replace it with its constituents. Otherwise, specializations might be tried if (say) a condition-action pair has previously led to improved performance but now appears unable to continue the progress.

In the following section, we give some substance to these remarks by considering two machine-learning procedures which have been applied to economic analysis.

---

[8]   This procedure was inspired by AM - a program developed by Douglas Lenat (1982) which by forming, evaluating, analogizing. specializing and generalizing a series of conjectures, succeeded in reinventing number theory.

Two Evolutionary Economic Procedures[9]

We all know that the process of Darwinian evolution depends on a supply of new combinations of characteristics, resulting from random variation and the natural selection of the combinations of characteristics, which give each species the best chance of surviving as a (perhaps modified) species. The identification of natural selection with the survival of the fittest is well established among biologists and lay persons alike.

All specifications of evolutionary mechanisms in economic modelling have some means of rewarding and reinforcing behaviour which is, in some well-defined sense, the fittest. It is usual for such behaviour to be determined by condition-action pairs, each of which constitutes a decision rule. Such rules assert that in states satisfying a given set of conditions, a particular set of actions should be taken. In general, conditions defined by any one rule are satisfied in several states and, conversely, several rules' conditions can be satisfied in one state. When several rules' conditions are satisfied in a given state, the 'strongest' rule is selected and its actions are taken. The 'strongest' rule is one which has accumulated the greatest strength as a result of its actions having yielded results which best satisfy some set of success criteria. For example, in a model where agents are assumed to be profit-maximizers, the strength of a rule could be the cumulative profits made in every period during which the rule determined an agent's action. More fundamental is the means of handling variation - the creation of new rules to compete with or supplant old rules. Some machine-learning procedures rely on random variation, whilst others do not. In this section, we consider one of each.

[9]   The particular implementations of the algorithms follow those reported by Goldberg (1989).

The Holland Classifier: Machine Learning as Genetics-Based Evolution

While the selection mechanism in biological evolution is easy to understand and model, the explanation of random variation was more difficult to understand until the combined efforts of quantum physicists and molecular biologists determined the structure of the DNA molecule.

The current understanding is that genetic information from each parent is encoded linearly in a four-character alphabet. Each linear encoding is embodied in a chromosome. To pass on the genetic information from parents to offspring, one chromosome from each parent is notionally laid alongside a chromosome from the other parent. The offspring's genetic code is then determined by choosing at each position the character from one parent's code at the corresponding position. The parent to donate the character for each position can be chosen at random. Alternatively, a dominance pattern (such as dark over fair hair) can ensure that at a given position one character, if present, is always given preference over another in the choice of characters for the offspring's genetic code. In this way, even nature's four-character genetic alphabet can create a very large number of possible combinations of characteristics.

In a series of papers, John Holland developed a representation of rules as a code enabling each rule to be treated as a chromosome. In Holland's terminology, these chromosome-like representations are called 'classifiers'. Sets of rules which govern behaviour are updated by 'mating' among the strongest classifiers and relatively high death rates for the weakest chromosomes.

As in biological genetics, chromosomes (classifiers) are strings of characters. In the simplest cases, the characters are drawn from a trinary alphabet - usually {1,0,#}. Each position in the string indicates the state of an environmental condition. If there is a '1' in a position, then the condition is true; if there is a '0' the condition is false, and a '#' indicates that the satisfaction of the condition is irrelevant. It might even be that two positions together represent a condition with four possible states - '00', '01', '10' or '11'. The state of the world is expressed by strings without the character '#'.

Rules have condition strings made up of the three characters. In deciding which rule should be used in given conditions, the condition string of each rule in the rulebase is matched against the string representing the state of the world. Several condition strings could match the state-of-the-world string. This multiplicity is made possible by the '#' character. If a state-of-the-world string is '011010', then all of the following condition strings will match it: '######', '#11##0', '0##01#', '011#10'. Only one of the rules can be chosen at each round.

The rule which is chosen will be that which makes the greatest 'bid'. The value of the bid made by each rule is related to rule 'strength'. Rules gain strength by receiving from the 'environment' a payoff whenever the rule is used. For example, if the rulebase represents the set of decision rules of a profit-maximizing firm, then whenever a rule is used the resulting profit (respectively loss) would be added to (respectively subtracted from) the number representing the strength of the rule.

In fact, things could be more complicated than this. It might be that a sequence of steps is required before any action is undertaken that brings a reward or penalty from the environment. A rule is chosen for the first step which alters the conditions and leads to the selection of a rule for the second step. The bid made by the successful second rule is then 'paid' to the first rule. That is, the value of the bid of the second rule is subtracted from its strength, while the strength of the first rule is increased by the same value. This process continues until there is an environmental reward or penalty which directly increases or diminishes the strength of the last rule to be used.

The procedure is called the 'bucket-brigade' algorithm. Its effect is to ensure that rules which indirectly lead to successful results are reinforced relative to unsuccessful rules. Those that lead indirectly to successful results through a number of different routes will be reinforced relative to those that are more specialized.

We have so far considered only the selection of rules. We turn now to the actions implied by rules.

In addition to a condition string, every rule has an action string. The actions implied by an action string depend on the characters filling each position. For example, the first position in an action string might be related to price-raising. Using the same alphabet as with the condition strings, a '1' might indicate a price rise by some specified amount, a '0' would then indicate no price rise, and a '#' would indicate that whatever action was taken last time should be taken this time.

The basic means of improving rulebases mimics genetic mechanisms in a Darwinian setting. Only the strongest rules are allowed to mate. Mating takes the form of a crossing-over of characters within the strings of each of the rules being mated. Suppose, for example, that the two rules being mated have condition strings '01##01' and '110#11'. Two offspring from these two rules would be formed by deciding at random whether to cross over the strings immediately after the first character and then the second character and so on. There is some probability of cross over. If that probability is p, then we would form two strings from the first character of each and then, with probability p, replace all of the following characters with the remaining characters of the other string. If cross-over were to occur at that point, then the two strings would be '010#11' and '11##01'. The algorithm then moves on to the second character and, with probability p, crosses over all the characters from the third onward, and so on until the last character is reached.

The general idea is always to mate the strongest rules in the rulebase in a way which produces offspring containing characteristics from each of the parents, and to remove the weakest rules altogether.

A Concept-Developing Algorithm

A very different approach to machine-learning has been reported by the present author (Moss, 1989).

My strategy was to form concepts by asserting and then testing conjectures about the relationships between decision variables and targets. Initially, an agent is assumed to have no information about these relationships. The initial information position is restricted to knowledge of the existence of the instruments and the targets. The procedure develops and investigates relationships which improve the values of the target variables.

For example, in a monopoly model the monopolist can be assumed to have two instruments - price and capacity - and one target - profit. In order to investigate the relationships between the instruments and the target, a simulated monopolist could assert that the relationship between price and profit is inverse. This assertion would be chosen at random in the sense that the assertion of a relationship between capacity and profit would have had an equal probability of being chosen as one between price and profit and, moreover, the assertion of a direct relationship would have had the same probability of being chosen as the assertion of an inverse relationship.

The conjecture of an inverse relationship would imply the testing of that relationship by reducing the value of the decision variable - in our example, the value of the price. If the price reduction was associated with an increase in profit, then the limit of that inverse relationship would be investigated by further price reductions until profits were reduced. If the initial price reduction was associated with a decline in profits, then a direct relationship would be conjectured and the limits investigated a series of price increases.

The next step would be to investigate relationships between other decision variables and targets in the same way. Once such relationships, if they exist, are uncovered, the effects of changes in some decision variables on the limits to the relationships between other instruments and targets are investigated. In this way, a set of increasingly complicated conjectures are formed and tested. If the tests confirm a conjecture, then that conjecture itself is used as an element in some further conjecture. In all cases, a successful test is one in which assuming the validity of the conjecture improves the values of target variables.

A Comparison of the Two Procedures

The question we must now face is how to assess the effectiveness of procedures in an area where economists in general have such little experience.

In order to take a first step in this direction, I developed two simulation models of a monopoly market. In one model, the decision rules of the monopolist are developed by means of Holland classifiers and associated genetic algorithms. In the other model, the decision rules of the monopolist were concerned only with the formation and testing of conjectures. Both of these models are implementations of the procedures described in the previous section. The market and technological environments were identical in the two models.

The environment common to the two models was entirely straightforward:

The decision variables in this model are price p and capacity K. Demand is determined entirely by price and the current output is the lesser of demand or capacity. Total cost is the sum of fixed capacity costs (5K in the cost equation) and direct costs (3q). Profit is then the difference between total revenue (pD) and total cost (C).

In all respects but one, this model is the standard, elementary textbook monopoly model. This model differs from the elementary textbook version in the discontinuity of the first derivative of the output function. This discontinuity was included in order to make simple incremental (or 'hill-climbing') algorithms inappropriate. The effect is to make much more difficult (and perhaps interesting) the problem of finding the optimal price-capacity configurations when the model which maps price and capacity into profit is not known.

In Figure 1 is depicted the tracks of price, capacity and profit relative to their optimal values during a simulation experiment with the conjecture-developing monopolist. The simulation experiment was abandoned after 38 cycles since the monopolist's profit was already within one per cent of the maximum.

The results with the genetics-based algorithm applied to the same monopolist are depicted in Figures 2 and 3. The uppermost line in Figure 2 represents the monopolist's capacity time series as a proportion of the optimal capacity value. As indicated in the figure, for some 1500 cycles of the simulation run beginning shortly after cycle 100, capacity fluctuated irregularly from nearly two and a half times the optimum to nearly three and a half times the optimum. At about the 1600th cycle, a new species of rule became dominant which reduced the capacity to a range from less than one and a half to less than twice the optimum. The effect on profit is easily seen in the lower line of Figure 2. As would be expected, the change in the capacity range improved the range of profit figures.

For the sake of completeness, I include as Figure 3 the time series for the ratio of price to its optimum in the genetic algorithm-based simulation run. The price fluctuated between 1.6 and 2.1 times its optimal value throughout the run. If new species of rule which reduced the level of prices had managed to get a foothold in the rulebase, then they would have come to dominate the old species and the price would fall.

In the fullness of time, it could reasonably be expected that capacity and price series would both come to fluctuate around their respective optima, so that the profit series would move closer to its optimum

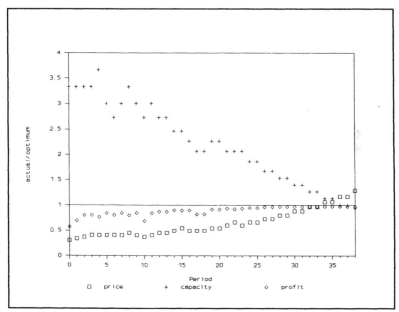

Figure 3.1   *The conjecturing monopolist's ratios of profit, capacity, and price to their optimal values*

with, perhaps, smaller fluctuations below the optimal value.

The temptation to attach importance to the difference in convergence rates of the two algorithms is understandable but not (yet) warranted. The Holland algorithm works well on complex environments where there are many local optima. The Moss algorithm has not even been tested on such environments.

One aspect of these two methods which would not change with increased model complexity is the information yielded by them. The genetic-evolutionary method yields information about the population of rules: the size of the population, the number of cross-overs, the number of mutations, the number of matings, etc. The conjecture-forming method can (and in the implementation reported here does) offer detailed explanations about the choice of actions and why new concepts are formed. An example of this explanatory power is given by the output from the program reproduced as Figure 4.

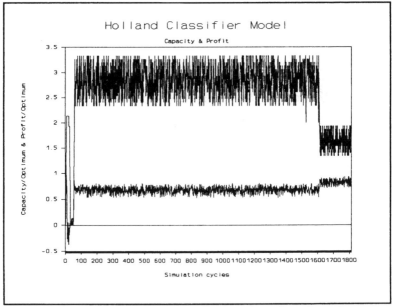

Figure 3.2   *The genetic monopolist's ratios of profit and capacity to their optimal values*

While there is obviously a lot of jargon in this output which is specific to the implementation, it is clear that the development of the monopolist's conjectures could hardly be more fully explained. At the very beginning, we are told that CONCEPT-3, which has been invented by the simulated monopolist, has been endorsed as 'found-valid'. This outcome entails the completion of a task set by the monopolist for himself (TASK-8) - the task having been to assess the validity of CONCEPT-3. As a result, a new task is warranted. This new task (TASK-9) is to decide to change the current capacity of the firm so that another new task (TASK-10) can be completed. This new task is to test the limits within which CONCEPT-3 is valid. The rest of the output reported in Figure 4 is describing and explaining the development of concepts involving variables which have been conjectured by the monopolist but are not themselves directly observable.

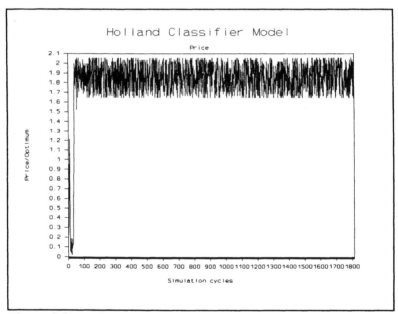

Figure 3.3 *The genetic monopolist's ratio of price to optimal price*

Conclusion

We have considered applications of two machine-learning procedures to a simple economic environment. One procedure makes it possible to find increasingly more appropriate behaviour in simulation runs of increasingly long length, but is not helpful in explaining the reasons for its behaviour. The other - at least in the model environment - also finds ever better behaviour (and in the particular environment does so orders of magnitude faster) but does so whilst providing detailed explanations of the reasons for behavioural changes.

Simple models obviously allow only for limited tests. It should be said that one of the advantages of approaches using Holland classifiers is that they entail a kind of parallelism in that they effectively assess several possible condition-action pairs simultaneously . Moreover, it is possible to prove theorems about the efficiency of machine-learning procedures based on these classifiers. The greater efficiency of the conjectural approach in the model monopoly environment must stem from the development of a set of rules which describe an efficient problem-solving strategy for that particular environment. Holland classifiers are of far more general applicability. Theorems about the results and relative efficiencies of computation procedures are attractive in that they enable one to distinguish between conceptual difficulties in programs and programming errors. Whether this attraction is offset by the lack of explication of results depends on the problem to hand.

In the end, I suspect that the choice of artificially-intelligent analytical technique will depend on whether the analyst is interested in outcome or process. If process is the interest, then the explanations facility will be important, as will the specification of the rules which guide learning. The value of such process models will not be the particular decision rules at which the model arrives, but rather the efficiency and plausibility of the process which gives rise to those rules.

If, as is the case with the simulation experiments described here, the process model is the more efficient in generating results, as well as describing the process of finding those results, it is hard to see

The concept called CONCEPT-3, which applies the operator INVERSE to the arguments (PROFIT-C CAPACITY-C), has been given the following endorsement:
(FOUND-VALID).
The task called TASK-8 has been completed by the application of ASSESS-VALIDITY to (CONCEPT-3).
Making TASK-9.
The purpose of this task is to apply the operator DECIDE to the arguments (CAPACITY-C 45.454544).
Making TASK-10.
The purpose of this task is to apply the operator TEST-LIMIT to the arguments (CONCEPT-3).
Before executing this task, the following condition must be satisfied:
(EXECUTED-TASK-P (QUOTE TASK-9)).
A new limiting value of concept CONCEPT-3 implying the relation INVERSE between PROFIT-C and CAPACITY-C has been found. The values are:
((PROFIT-C . 514.99835) (CAPACITY-C . 45)).
(CONCEPT-3).

Making concept VARIABLE-CONCEPT-1.
This concept specifies an INTERMEDIATE-VARIABLE-C.
The operator applied by VARIABLE-CONCEPT-1 is:
LIMIT-VALUES.
The arguments are: (CONCEPT-3 PROFIT-C).
Making concept CONCEPT-4.
This concept specifies a RELATION-C.
The operator applied by CONCEPT-4 is: INVERSE.
The arguments are: (VARIABLE-CONCEPT-1 PRICE-C).

Figure 3.4   *Output as the model finds valid intermediate concepts and relationships*

what objection could be offered by economists who are not interested in the process per se. It is just that the experiments demonstrate both that learning in conditions of scarce information-processing capacity can lead to the results economists have long predicted by assuming unlimited information-processing capacity. Provided that the learning procedures specified can also be applied to models which have previously been intractable to conventional analytical techniques, then there is an unambiguous gain. If the extension of the conventional results to complex economies entails the loss of explanation of how the results are achieved, then the results themselves might be less convincing to those whose policies economists seek to influence. In that case, there must be some ambiguity as to the gain.

Finally, we note that both of the approaches considered here involve the evolution of decision rules. These are not simple rules of thumb. They are descriptions of arbitrarily complex decision-making procedures. My own concern with process led me to use rules and machine-learning algorithms that are readily comprehensible to the user of the implementations of the algorithms. The concern of Marimon, McGrattan and Sargent was not so much with the process as to demonstrate that a process exists which confirms the results of conventional, rational-expectations theory. Nonetheless, their demonstration relied on rule-based behaviour so that, fundamentally, their work is within the purview of Simon's theory of procedural rationality.

It is clearly too early to suggest that we are now all behavioural economists. It is not too early to suggest that the fundamental differences between behavioural and neoclassical economics vanish once we turn to the analysis of complex economic environments. The differences that remain are concerned with degrees of aggregation rather than analytical fundamentals.

4. AI Modelling Techniques: The Emergence of a Support Framework for Modelling Complex Behaviour in Economics

John Rae and Martin L. Reynolds

Introduction

In this paper we explore rule-based modelling techniques drawn from the areas of artificial intelligence and cognitive psychology. We shall argue and illustrate that such techniques can be usefully employed in the study of economic behaviour. The focus is upon illustrating the process of developing computer-based models and assessing their value in the study of complex economic behaviour. No attempt is made in this paper to prioritize particular modelling techniques. The primary aim is to indicate feasible and interesting directions for future research.

We discuss the motivation for a non-traditional approach and how and where such AI techniques may be applied to help develop our understanding of the nature of adaptive behaviour. However, whilst there is a behavioural emphasis underpinning the discussion in this paper, it is also argued that these relatively new concepts and techniques complement the orthodox framework of neoclassical economics rather than challenge its validity.

Modelling Economic Behaviour: Motivation for Change

There is, in economics, what might be called the literature of discontent. The writings of a body of economists who are at once both fascinated and disappointed at the 'inhuman' treatment of economic actors in the task of decision-making. Much of this discontent has been expressed in the context of the theory of the firm, and in particular that part of economics known as the behavioural theory of the firm.

The elegance and ingenuity of the neoclassical framework of analysis contrasts sharply with the desire to characterize realistically economic behaviour. The 'black box' approach to modelling in neoclassical economics fails to consider the nature of the underlying processes that characterize human behaviour. To raise the lid of the black-box and to look inside has been the goal of behavioural economists; the reluctance of neoclassical economics to look inside, along with the justification for not doing so, is clearly the foundation for much of the criticism of the neoclassical approach. By not exploring the process of decision-making, for whatever reason, neoclassical economics maintains some semblance of order in analytical methods. However, this order is removed once processes are considered. Mathematical analysis is typically replaced by description and simulation methods, which are often viewed as less powerful means of analysis. Thus it is not surprising that in the literature of discontent there exists an ambivalent attitude to neoclassical methods both fascination and disappointment; indeed it is testimony to the undeniable elegance and limitations of neoclassical theory.

It is important to recognize the contribution of the neoclassical paradigm to our understanding of the problems of efficient resource allocation. The framework of analysis is powerful, and has resulted in robust and general predictions about economic behaviour. A good example is the considerable progress made in the modelling of decision-making behaviour under uncertainty. It is not our purpose here to challenge the findings of neoclassical economics. Instead, following the work of Simon, we question the validity of maintaining the assumption of substantively rational behaviour in complex and uncertain environments. We wish to highlight that there exists a range of tools and techniques in disciplines like artificial intelligence and cognitive psychology that enable economists to focus on aspects of procedural rationality in the modelling of economic behaviour.

In sum, it is argued that it is necessary to develop a means of modelling decision processes and adaptive behaviour, not as an alternative to the neoclassical framework of analysis, but as a complementary methodology. In this way we can extend the boundaries of economic analysis and increase its contribution to enhancing our understanding of human behaviour.

Relaxing the Assumption of Substantive Rationality: Some Implications for Economic Analysis

The work of Herbert Simon suggests that the concept of substantive rationality is of limited value for the analysis of complex economic behaviour for two (related) reasons. First, it is argued that the information-processing capacity of economic agents is limited. For example, there is extensive experimental work (see Hogarth (1980); Kahneman and Tversky (1984)) that supports the view that cognitive simplification mechanisms are an important feature of decision-making behaviour. Heiner (1983) has also used this argument as a basis for predicting behaviour in complex and uncertain task domains. He argues that the presence of a 'C-D gap' arising from limited information-processing capacity results in the emergence of regularities in human behaviour in the form of heuristic decision rules.

A second difficulty with the substantive rationality concept is that there is no meaningful distinction made between different classes of decision in terms of their impact upon the process of decision-making. This contrasts with the views taken by researchers in other disciplines. For example, in the business and management literature an important distinction is made between operational and strategic decisions - a distinction regarded as essential to the understanding of business behaviour (see, for example, Johnson and Scholes (1989)).

The distinction between substantive and procedural rationality raises significant questions about the purpose and focus of economics. There is much use of the terms 'behaviour', 'modelling of behaviour', 'rational behaviour' and 'explanation and prediction of behaviour' within economics. This, on the surface, would appear to agree with Marshall's (1920) Principles definition of economics:

> ... the study of mankind in the ordinary business of life ... connected with the attainment and with the use of the material requisites of well being.

It is open to debate whether much more than a superficial similarity exists between Marshall's definition of economics and what academic economists teach and research today. Economics has concentrated attention within a narrow band of 'man's character', providing only a partial (and perhaps misleading) description of the 'business of life'.

Are we making an unreasonable challenge in suggesting that economics is concerned with only a small subset of possible human behaviour - that which is termed 'substantively rational behaviour'? By focusing upon a subset of human behaviour, which lends itself (by coincidence?) to rigorous mathematical treatment, economics has lost some of the richness implied by a reasonable interpretation of Marshall's definition of economics.

It is also interesting to consider the influence of the tools of economic analysis upon both the scope and the formulation of economic research in the latter half of the twentieth century. Koopmans (1957) in his third essay, 'The Interaction of Tools and Problems in Economics', argues that:

> quite properly the definition (of economics) specifies only the problems to be studied, and not the, tools of observation and analysis to be applied to these problems. In principle tools have a servant's status .... The tools that should be developed for future use depend on the precise nature of the problems that seem most likely to be demanding or promising further answers (pp. 169-170).

Therein lies a central aim of this paper, an investigation into the adaptation and use of a particular set of tools for the analysis of the 'ordinary business of life'. One area that we believe is 'promising further answers' is that of adaptive behavioural economics.

Moving Towards Models of Procedural Rationality

There is no universally accepted approach to the development of models that examine aspects of procedural rationality. In economics there has been some progress towards developing such a framework for behavioural research (see, for example, Gilad and Kaish (1986)). However, the diversity of styles and approaches to behavioural research suggests that a considerable amount of work remains to be done.

Research into the modelling of the processes that characterize behaviour in complex problem domains requires consideration of a number of issues:

(a)   What is an appropriate theoretical language for modelling process phenomena?

(b)   What aspects of the behaviour of systems are to be the subject of analysis for the purpose of developing conclusions about process aspects of behaviour?

(c)   How are we to capture an understanding of the detailed aspects of the process characteristics of decision-making?

A common approach to process modelling within AI and cognitive psychology research is the view (though by no means universally accepted) that behaviour can best be analysed by trying to model and reproduce it. Often reproduction is achieved by means of the use of powerful computer simulation models.

Whilst Cyert and March (1963) introduced the importance of computer simulation in economics, they were not able to develop a structured approach to computer-based modelling of complex processes. They did not of course have the benefit of over two decades of AI research - nor did they have access to the powerful modelling environments available today. Arguably, a major problem with the work of Cyert and March was the failure to establish important conceptual links between the form of the natural language they adopted (computer simulation) and the behavioural phenomena that underpinned their theory. Central to what will be argued in this paper is the idea of translation, since all modelling involves translation - one translates that which one senses as being important into another form, the model. Languages are central to this process of translation, and failing to consider the properties of the language of expression being used may result in a poor translation devoid of essential meaning. In other words, the model misrepresents reality because the language is inadequately expressing meaning.

Computer scientists have recognized the significance of language when designing artificial high-level computer languages. Such languages are problem-oriented, their linguistic structure makes each language more suitable for the purpose for which it was designed.

Mathematics is a language used in economics as a formal means of expressing observed behaviour. The richness of the observed behaviour is translated, that is, mathematized, by a restatement of the observations into magnitudes and relations. The rules of mathematics allow manipulation of statements in order to derive theorems, that is, new expressions of behaviour. There are clearly a number of economic variables that are not easily expressed using the conventional language of mathematics that characterizes neoclassical economics. Arguably, it is the behavioural processes within the 'black box' that economics has found so difficult to faithfully translate into a mathematical formalism.

Simon (1978) alludes to the problems of language choice in a discussion of the use of mathematics in the social sciences. For encoding verbal forms of communication:

> standard modes of mathematization seem to lose most of the content of what is going on .... True, abstraction is at the heart of science, but not abstraction that loses the essential data (pp 162).

Mathematics is a vehicle that allows the consequences of various assumptions to be derived in a 'mechanical' manner by the application of rules; without these rules the consequences are not obvious to see. In this sense there is no difference between a computer program and mathematics. The program contains a transparent set of rules that are applied in a 'mechanical' manner to the data, in order to derive the consequential information.

The choice of an appropriate formal language for representing procedurally rational models of behaviour in economics is not a trivial issue. Below we describe a particular formalism of computer simulation models that have their origin in AI and cognitive psychology. The formalism is known as a production system model (PS). As will be demonstrated later, PS models are of particular interest because of their association with the information-processing theory of human behaviour developed by Newell and Simon (1972). A second issue concerns the nature of the phenomena to be captured and modelled within a framework focused upon issues of procedural rationality. Once again, the research findings of other disciplines are of relevance here, and it seems appropriate to take advantage of synergies from the studies of decision-making behaviour in these disciplines. Some common areas of concern emerge in the AI and cognitive psychology literature. For example, there is extensive coverage of procedural aspects of behaviour relating to knowledge and reasoning strategies (particularly in uncertain environments); learning and adaptive behaviour; strategic and gaming behaviour; heuristic decision rules and recipes; stability of system behaviour; the role of multiple goals and conflict resolution strategies and so on. In this paper, we shall restrict ourselves to illustrating the modelling of learning and adaptive behaviour.

The final issue we noted above is concerned with the problem of how we obtain insight into behavioural processes that characterize decision-making in complex environments. Within a procedurally rational framework of analysis, decision-making is non-trivial and the result of considerable deliberation. Work in the field of AI and cognitive psychology has made a significant contribution to improving our understanding of intelligent behaviour through the direct observation of decision-making processes. A number of behavioural researchers (see, for example, Gilad and Kaish (1986)) have argued that economists should be concerned with observing the actual processes of behaviour. This seems an important feature of research that is focused upon the procedural aspects of the behaviour of complex systems.

Observing human behaviour is not without problems. Once again, if we look to the AI and cognitive psychology literatures it is possible to find support mechanisms for tackling this issue. For example, with respect to the collection and analysis of detailed behavioural process data, the technique of verbal protocol analysis has widespread use in the field of cognitive psychology. Similarly, with respect to the observation of human behaviour, the use of experiments is a common feature of the research methods in AI and cognitive psychology (see the paper by Hey and Reynolds in this volume).

In sum, we have highlighted some of the issues that need to be addressed by economists concerned with developing process models of behaviour. There are merits in taking an inter-disciplinary perspective towards the development of process models in economics. The disciplines of AI and cognitive psychology provide a number of support tools for developing process models of behaviour in economics. The potential for synergy between AI and economics is the result of the convergence of a number of trends; this convergence has rapidly accelerated during the last decade. These trends reflect factors both internal and external to the discipline of economics. The most significant of these trends are: the maturation of AI techniques and their successful application in other fields (notably in expert systems); the increased opportunities for applying AI techniques through the availability of powerful and affordable computers; the growing acceptance of the value of adopting an inter-disciplinary approach to the study of economic behaviour; and a recognition (particularly by behavioural economists) of the opportunities for modelling complex decision processes using computer-based simulation techniques.

In the remaining sections of this paper we give examples of how these support mechanisms may be applied.

Rule-Based Simulation: Production System Models:

Rule-based models are often referred to as production models. A production is an alternative name for a rule. Before examining a particular adaptive model we shall explain the basics of rule-based or production system models.

Before considering actual models, it is necessary to outline in greater detail the structure of a PS. Two simple examples will suffice to demonstrate the principles involved. A rule structure is symbolic, that is, observed entities, variables and values are represented by symbols. These productions are a series of condition-action pairs of the type C = > A, where C is the set of conditions {C1......Cn} and A is a sequence of actions {A1.....An}. Thus there might exist the following productions (P1, P2 and P3):

P1 (A B (CC)) -> (A (BCC))
P2 (BCC)   -> (B (BBCC))
P3 (A B)   -> (C (BCC))

The letters within the brackets represent symbol structures; the left hand side (LHS) conditions are compared with the working memory (WM) contents to find matches. The WM is the input-output buffer where the results of rule processing reside and/or exogenously determined values are made available to the model. The WM may contain the following:

WM = { (A B) B }

Thus, starting from P1, the LHS of each production is compared to the WM. It can be seen that only P3 can be instantiated, that is, find a match between the LHS of the rule and the working memory contents. The right hand side (RHS) action is therefore executed. The action of P3 is to add to the contents of WM, which now contains:

WM = { C (BCC) (A B) B }

This completes one recognize-act cycle. The cycle now begins again and, assuming a very simplistic resolution strategy that is, which rule is to fire if more than one rule is instantiated, P2 is chosen over P3 as it is the first production to find a match. The action again is to add to the WM, which now contains:

WM = { B (BBCC) C (BCC) (A B) }

This completes the second recognize-act cycle, which is sufficient for our purposes. In this very simple example only additions have been made to the WM. It is also forward-chaining in that it has operated by first the LHS finding a match and then the RHS action being performed. Below we shall consider another strategy, that of backward-chaining.

Using such structures, various behavioural models may be constructed by the formation of appropriate rules. Such models may be performance models, that is, testing hypotheses on the basis of a static, unchanging rulebase, or they may be adaptive, that is, learning models. Learning can be simulated in a number of ways. In order to be more precise, the concept of learning in this respect means knowledge acquisition, that is, the acquiring of new symbolic information and the ability to apply that new knowledge in an effective manner. Thus this may entail one, or more, of the following possibilities: creating new rules, amending current rules to become more specific and therefore more restricted in application, generalization by making conditions less restrictive, and combining frequently sequentially used pairs of rules.

The range of information-processing models that have been developed is quite extensive: Simon (1979a) provides a survey of such developments (there are 170 referenced works). The interested reader may wish to consult this article for a more detailed discussion of the developments than is possible in the constraints of this paper.

Let us briefly consider a backward-chaining system. If we represent productions by letting each knowledge element in the list structure above be represented by tokens, that is, TK1, TK2.....TKN, then we may have seven productions as below:

P1 (TK1 TK2) -> (TK6)
P2 (TK3 TK4) -> (TK7)
P3 (TK5)   -> (TK8)
P4 (TK2 TK7) -> (TK9)
P5 (TK6 TK8) -> (TK11)
P6 (TK7 TK5) -> (TK10)
P7 (TK9 TK10)-> (TK11)

Such productions represent the behaviour of the subject. For the system to function a goal is required let the goal be to achieve the establishment of the truth of the hypothesis that given certain facts TK11 may be inferred from them. The facts reside in WM and are symbol structures which reflect elements of the problem environment. The working memory may contain the following facts:

$$WM = \{TK3\ TK4\ TK2\ TK5\}$$

The goal is to establish whether such facts provide LHS 'evidence' to enable TK11 to be inferred, that is, can either production P5 or P7 be instantiated on the basis of the contents of WM? The process of backward-chaining is such that the following recursive process is used:

P5 or P7 have TK11 as a RHS element;
     therefore, can either 'fire'?
Using P5 - are facts TK6 and TK8 in WM?
     no - then recurse - TK6 is RHS of P1, therefore, can P1 'fire'?
     no - TK1 is not in WM - then recurse,
fail, because TK1 is not in any RHS = > stop.
Using P7 - are facts TK9 and TK10 in WM?
     no - then recurse - TK9 is RHS of P4,
          therefore, can P4 'fire'?
     no - TK2 is in WM but TK7 is not - then recurse - TK7 is RHS of P2, therefore, can P2 'fire'?
     yes - TK3 and TK4 are in WM = > place TK7 in WM,
WM = {TK7 TK3 TK4 TK2 TK5}
     therefore, can P4 'fire'?
     yes - TK2 and TK7 are in WM = > place TK9 in WM,
WM = {TK9 TK7 TK3 TK4 TK2 TK5}
therefore, can P7 'fire'?
     no - because TK9 is, but TK10 is not in WM - then recurse,
     -TK10 is the RHS of P6, therefore, can P6 'fire'?
     yes - TK7 and TK5 are in WM = > place TK10 in WM,

WM = {TK10 TK9 TK7 TK3 TK4 TK2 TK5}
    therefore, can P7 'fire'?
    yes - TK9 and TK10 are in WM = > place TK11 in WM,

WM = {TK11 TK10 TK9 TK7 TK3 TK4 TK2 TK5}

TK11 is shown to be a fact that can be inferred as true.

Learning: The Market Entrant Model

In this model we shall examine the means by which a hypothetical firm evolves successful strategies. (Rae and Reynolds (1983), Rae (1987) and Reynolds (1989)).

Briefly, the situation is that of an entrant into a product market; the entrant has to compete for market share against a number of existing firms which have formed a cartel, thus essentially we are concerned with modelling a duopoly situation.

This model poses the question: what strategic behaviour would evolve if an entrepreneur faced an uncertain and dynamically changing market with the goals of achieving satisfactory profit and satisfactory market share, but had no predetermined behavioural rules?

The entrant model has only one initial rule which is used upon entering the market. The rule is: price at the prevailing price level. It has no other predetermined rule and it may only use this entrance rule once. Thereafter it must discover rules.

Such an approach opens up a new area of enquiry in economics. Given particular environmental conditions and a procedurally rational learning mechanism, what economic behaviour will develop? The PS framework will describe precisely the learned behaviour in the form of rules.

It needs to be clearly understood that these rules did not exist before the model was run on the computer. OPS4, the modelling language employed (Forgy and McDermott (1976)), is written as an interpreter in the LISP language, and as such has the capability to generate, under supervision, new program code.

This new program code is in the form of rules of behaviour, that is, new production rules. In order to make clear this mechanism we shall briefly divert attention to the programming techniques before analysing in detail the entrant model.

Learning and the New Entrant Model

Given that a PS rule is of the following form:

$$(C1, C2,...CN) -> (A1, A2,...AN)$$

learning can involve one or more of the following possible types of rule adaptation.

Type	Effect
One	Create/Replace LHS and RHS
Two	Replace LHS only
Three	Replace RHS only
Four	Replace some LHS elements
Five	Replace some RHS elements

Table 4.1 *Types of rule adaptation*

The LHS and RHS refer to the left hand side condition elements and right hand side actions, respectively. Thus the rulebase is changed in order to display adaptive behaviour by one or more of the above types. The model of the entrant employs types one, two and three. The major problem for the PS modeller is to develop the mechanism by which the rules are altered or developed. In this entrant model a very simplistic mechanism is adopted.

This mechanism is sufficient to allow the entrant to adapt

satisfactorily to the uncertain and dynamically changing market. Before considering in detail the adaptive mechanism and results, we will examine the external environment.

External Environment

The external environment consists of the market conditions and the entrant's information system, as in the previous simple behavioural model.

We shall consider the market conditions first of all. The market was designed to provide a very complex but realistic external environment. The market had to change both dynamically and in response to price. The market demand function therefore had two components; we shall take each component in turn, starting with the dynamic element.

A concept commonly found in marketing literature is the product life-cycle hypothesis. This states that a product goes through a number of stages throughout its life. In the period in which the product is regarded as new, that is, in the youthful stage, the market demand consists of mainly those purchasers who are consumer leaders. The market conditions change as the product 'catches on' and also becomes cheaper to purchase. In this stage, the growth stage, total demand is growing rapidly over time. This phase cannot last. The product market eventually stabilizes to a more or less constant level of demand. This is the mature product stage, which may in time develop into old age with declining total market demand.

The product life-cycle hypothesis is incorporated into the model by the following functional form, which is in fact a logistic curve:

$$\text{Market demand} = \frac{a}{1 + be^{-xt}} \tag{4.1}$$

a, b and x are market parameters, a = 1000, b = 14.3, x = 0.03 and t = time period.

This is the basis for the growth of the market over time. The entrant has no 'innate' knowledge of the shape of the market growth curve.

There are possible shifts in the market growth curve according to whether the firms have priced at, below or above the expected market price. It was assumed that consumers have expectations of a market price for the product, and that this expectation alters over time. The basis for these expectations is the expected price at maturity weighted exponentially. This is considered quite realistic, as normally one expects that new products are at first relatively expensive, in order that the development costs of the product may be recouped from the consumer leaders, and that later the price will decline to some long-run 'normal' level. However, should the price deviate from these expectations then, depending on the direction of the deviation, more or less consumers are attracted to the product at that time. Thus the product may suddenly appear relatively cheap or relatively expensive in relation to the current value of the expected price.

In order to accommodate the price expectations element, the market growth curve has been weighted by the following function:

$$\text{Weight} = \frac{(N + 1)\ Pe \exp^{.5/t}}{(Pc_t + Pent_t)} \tag{4.2}$$

Pe = Price expected at maturity
N = Number in cartel
t = Time period
Pc_t = Cartel price at t
$Pent_t$ = Entrant price at t

This weight tends to the value of one if the general price level approximates the current expected price level. The current price is the price expected at maturity, weighted by an exponential form which tends to the value of one over time. Thus the price that is expected eventually tends to the maturity level. If the general price level is, for example, below that expected at any particular time in the product life-cycle, the logistic curve is shifted upwards, producing an overall increase in market demand at that time.

The firms involved have no knowledge of the market environment apart from the sales results which provide feedback to decisions. The share of the total market demand that each firm obtains is proportional to their relative prices. Thus if both cartel and entrant price equally, the demand is shared equally.

The pricing rule of the cartel is very simple: it is the previous price adjusted for the market share that it achieved plus a random element. This rule is mechanically applied each period without any adaptation and the entrant does not know the pricing policy of the cartel.

The entrant thus faces a complex market environment about which it has no information other than the results that comprise the feedback via its information system. These results are concerned with the sales achieved, stock levels, profitability, cost of production and price level. Its objectives are twofold: to gain and hold a market share and to achieve a satisfactory level of profitability. The entrant is assumed to prefer more profit to less, providing it maintains a proportional market share. The cost conditions for all the firms are identical and consist of two components: production costs and the storage costs of stockholding. These are deducted from profits at the end of each period. Thus the two decision variables are the price of the product and the level of production.

Adaptive Mechanism

The model was allowed to run for 400 periods in order that the entrant may experience all aspects of the product life-cycle and develop appropriate behavioural rules. It was anticipated that the rate of rule development would follow a pattern which responded positively to the extent of uncertainty encountered in the market. Uncertainty in this context means the unknown extent to which the market was growing and the unknown pricing policy of the cartel.

In the early periods the market is growing quickly as the product gains acceptance, thus one would expect a high degree of learning to take place, as measured by the frequency of change in the production rules. Later, as the market reaches maturity and demand is more stable, one would expect less change in the rulebase. In fact this is precisely what occurred, as the discussion of the results in a later section will reveal.

In an earlier section, learning was categorized according to the degree of change of the rulebase (see Table 1). In the entrant model, types one, two and three occurred. This learning was achieved via the feedback from the entrant's accounting information system. Information provided by the system enabled market share and profitability to be monitored and compared to previous performance. Also, the level of stocks, the production and storage of which formed the costs for the firm, was monitored and adjusted via three rules which were given and not learned. The rules simply adjusted production up or down according to past sales performance and current levels of stocks, the aim being to provide a safety margin of stocks of about 10% in relation to previous sales figures. The rule used here is in keeping with the general philosophy of Cyert and March's (1963) general model using a minimum and maximum limit on inventories relative to the size of sales. Indeed, much of the model outlined draws upon the behavioural theory of the firm for the characterization of the entrant's behaviour.

Learning was concerned with the recognition of market conditions not previously encountered, as described by price and sales movements, and the consequent development of an appropriate response, that is, RHS action. Appropriate in relation to achieving the entrant's objectives. Thus, the entrant must be able to evaluate the success of rules and if necessary avoid repetition of unsuccessful rules.

One element is missing from the description of the model at present, and until that is included it is not a well-structured problem. Within the model we have the means to produce new rules, but we have not yet declared how the entrant may know the solution to the problem; that is, a means of testing the effects of the rules to determine whether they are satisfactory or not. Performance is assessed on the basis of sales performance for each rule constructed. If a rule is connected with a fall in sales in three consecutive firings, as recorded by the information system, then it is considered to be unsuccessful. It is removed from the rulebase and replaced by another.

However, before the performance of the rules can be assessed, they must first be created. The creation process depends upon the ability of information-processing models to pattern match, that is, to compare the contents of WM with the LHS conditions of the rules. If a match is found then the rule is said to be instantiated and may be fired; if no match is found the model will halt for the simple reason that it has no way to respond. This lack of a match may be used by a modeller to create a rule. In order to do this one needs only to specify which part(s) of the external environment are pertinent to the model's behaviour. In the context of the entrant model, this means observe what price and sales conditions presently exist and their relation to previous conditions. These observations then form the basis of the LHS conditions' they are encoded in symbol structures which describe the variables and their relationships, the permutations of which have not occurred previously. Had they occurred previously, a rule would have existed in the rulebase and could have been used.

This simple mechanism provides a basis for the recognition of new environmental conditions for which some appropriate action must be developed. For simplicity in the model the adaptive mechanism was instructed to extract certain elements from the external environment. However, this is not essential since the model could be so constructed to learn about what elements in the environment to filter out; again the mechanism would require a means of assessing satisfactory performance in this context.

The next task for the entrant, having formed the LHS of the rule, is to develop an appropriate response for the new environmental conditions which are described by the LHS. This requires that the entrant be able to select an action and also remember the action selected. Let us consider what actions are open to the entrant.

The two decision variables are production and price, the production decision rule has been dealt with earlier and takes no part in the following discussion. Pricing decisions however, can only be one of three possibilities: raise price, lower price or keep price constant. Within the raise/lower price option there are infinite possibilities, but for simplicity the alteration was confined to ten per cent in either direction. This kind of behaviour was chosen to provide a standard rule for pricing decisions of the type observed by Cyert and March (1963). A possibility, not explored in the present model, is to include search mechanisms to adapt the standard pricing rule should it prove unsatisfactory. The percentage change would thereby be adjusted should ten per cent be found to be inappropriate.

The problem for the entrant is to search for the most appropriate conditions in which to use the standard decision rule options. That is, to raise or lower the price by ten per cent or, alternatively, leave the price unaltered. Thus at all times there is active search for satisfactory rules via feedback through the entrant's information system. There are a limited number of possibilities that can exist in the product market, in fact nine in all. These are shown in Table 2.

For simplicity these ignore the range of movement and take into account only the direction of movement. Thus it is very unlikely that possibilities (3), (6) and (9) will in fact occur. Development of this model could certainly take the direction of evolving pertinent range values for the recognition of significant movements of market variables. In total there are a possible twenty-seven rules the entrant could build, that is, nine possible LHS market conditions to recognize, and three RHS pricing possibilities for each of those nine. In fact, during the four hundred period run of the model, fifteen of these rules were constructed.

1) PRICE CONSTANT AND SALES INCREASED

2) PRICE CONSTANT AND SALES DECREASED

3) PRICE CONSTANT AND SALES CONSTANT

4) PRICE DECREASE AND SALES INCREASED

5) PRICE DECREASE AND SALES DECREASED

6) PRICE DECREASE AND SALES CONSTANT
7) PRICE INCREASED AND SALES INCREASED

8) PRICE INCREASED AND SALES DECREASED

9) PRICE INCREASED AND SALES CONSTANT

Table 4.2   *Possible market conditions*

The entrant was given no innate 'understanding' of what a 'good' rule is, that could only come about via experience in the marketplace. To begin with the only method the entrant has of managing a new market situation, for which it has no current rule of behaviour, is to construct a rule and randomly choose an RHS action. It will be recalled that the entrant constructed the LHS condition statement from the current market state combined with recent historical market conditions, obtained from the firm's information system. It then randomly selects an action, from those at its disposal, and this forms the RHS of the rule. The complete rule is then stored in the rulebase and is subsequently utilized.

Once a market condition has been recognized and formed into an LHS, then assessment of the performance of the RHS actions can begin. This employs feedback about the success of the current version of the rule vis-à-vis sales and should it be unsatisfactory, that is, sales fall on each occasion when the rule is used in three consecutive firings, then it is excised (removed) from the rulebase and a new version constructed. The new version has the same LHS but a new RHS. The RHS is an action chosen from the remaining possible actions, that is, excluding those previously used with this LHS, unless all three possibilities have been used, in which case all are open to selection again. The initial selection of the RHS actions is random because there is no a priori best choice for the entrant. The process is one which over time selects decision rules which have the capacity to survive in a range of market conditions, thus successful rules are robust rules.

One such robust rule is shown below:

G211
IF
PRICE LAST PERIOD WAS REDUCED BY 10%; AND

SALES HAVE INCREASED
THEN
HOLD PRICE CONSTANT THIS PERIOD

This particular rule was built quite early on in the simulation, period seven, and remained active for twenty-six periods, firing on some nine occasions.

Table 3 summarizes the rule types - of the possible twenty-seven rules, in fact only fifteen were constructed. Not all of these rules were in existence at one time, and the same type of rule went by a different name at different times. The rule G211, for example, is type 8; it was first constructed in period 7 and eventually proved unsatisfactory and was excised. However, that same type of rule was later constructed on three more occasions and so for a total of 254 periods such a rule existed.

In all, thirty-eight rules were constructed comprising these fifteen types, and thirty-two of these were at some point excised from the rulebase. The uncertainty in the environment ensured that the rule base did change and adapt over time, and it did so in proportion to the degree of change in the environment. The first one hundred periods were characterized by a great deal of change in the environment, as this corresponded to the youth and growth stages in market demand. During this time fourteen rules were developed, whereas in each of the three following one hundred periods a consistent eight rules per one hundred periods was constructed. The initial turbulence of the market environment resulted in the entrant's rapid attempts to find satisfactory rules, whereas in later stages a more stable environment reduced the need for adaptive search behaviour.

The process of adaptation in the entrant's behaviour is one of trial and error. This rather unsophisticated strategy actually performed satisfactorily, as Figure 1 shows. The entrant did gain and hold a proportional market share on the basis of simple pattern recognition and feedback control via its information system. This display of very simple-minded search behaviour is quite reasonable under the circumstances - the entrant does not know what satisfactory decision rules are a priori and so experimentation must take place.

Furthermore, given that the market environment is both competitive and dynamically changing, previously unsatisfactory decision rules may later become satisfactory decision rules. Thus to banish such rules permanently from the rule-base, on the basis of having failed once, may prove unwise.

Clearly, rules which followed the strategy of not changing price proved most successful, and hence survived the greatest number of periods. On the other hand, raising price was in general an unsuccessful policy which resulted in very short lifespans for such rules. At the end of the four hundred period run of the model, not one rule for raising price remained in the rulebase. This is precisely what one would expect at this time, because the market is no longer growing and any increase in price is unlikely to meet with a favourable response.

Rule Type	[LHS CONDITIONS] Price Change	Sales Change	[RHS] Action (Price)	Periods Survived	Number of Firings
1	NONE	UP	UP	65	11
2	NONE	UP	SAME	28	11
3	NONE	UP	DOWN	301	67
4	NONE	DOWN	UP	27	6
5	NONE	UP	SAME	225	57
6	NONE	DOWN	DOWN	127	44
7	DOWN	UP	UP	24	6
8	DOWN	UP	SAME	254	56
9	DOWN	UP	DOWN	115	43
10	DOWN	DOWN	****	***	**
11	DOWN	DOWN	SAME	354	6
12	DOWN	DOWN	****	***	**
13	UP	UP	****	***	**
14	UP	UP	SAME	275	12
15	UP	UP	DOWN	118	1
16	DOWN	DOWN	UP	6	6
17	DOWN	DOWN	SAME	136	18
18	DOWN	DOWN	DOWN	247	62

* Not constructed

Table 4.3   *Rule types*

The entrant model is thus characterised by bounded rationality, simple minded search behaviour, satisfactory performance and conformity to the principles of an information processing system. The decision rules require only five chunks of information in STM, well within the 'magic number' findings, and a limited number of simple EIP'S are sufficient to generate the behaviour. The model also provides an answer to question of: what kind of behaviour develops given a particular external environment and a learning mechanism? The behaviour is clearly expressed in the rules the system constructs. For this particular model the firm discovered robust strategies that were satisfactory.

In particular, it was discovered that the better strategies were decrease price or hold price constant. If one totals the periods survived for all rules and examines the percentage of periods survived for each strategy one obtains the following rough measure of robustness:

hold price constant.......... 55.35%
lower price.................. 39.4%
raise price.................. 5.25%

Figure 4.1   *Measure of robustness*

Conclusion

The philosophy of the research programme advocated in this paper is quite simply as follows: if we recognize the importance of the process of decision-making, we must also recognize the human capacity for handling information and the associated human limitations. In doing so we have broken down the barrier between economics and psychology which substantively rational utility theory had constructed.

I. Fisher, in 1892, wrote in his doctoral dissertation:

> ... This foisting of psychology on Economics seems to me inappropriate and vicious....

It is nearly one century later and the case is still being argued; 'vicious' the human information-processing theory (HIP) is not; however, economics has progressed during the last century largely without the benefit of psychological tenets and the result is the generally impoverished state of behavioural theory. On the other hand, HIP is undoubtedly a challenge to neoclassical economics in so far that it points to the inadequacies of the traditional methods. However, rather than approach the classical edifice in an adversarial manner, it is important to realize that the HIP behavioural approach complements the classical theories by providing a procedurally rational modelling tool in an essential and relatively neglected area.

In our enthusiasm for 'slum clearance' in the seventies we destroyed many fine Victorian and Edwardian buildings which we now in the nineties might, with a different perspective, appreciate. In our enthusiasm for mathematical rigour, let us not make the same mistake and overlook the elegance of earlier behavioural economics. We now have the instruments and methods to give substance to many descriptive processes in the 'ordinary business of life'. The richness and diversity of human behaviour is awaiting our ingenuity to comprehend and model it; can we afford to resist the challenge?

5. Strategic Decision-Making: Orthodox Theory versus Artificial Intelligence Approaches

A. Romeo and Scott Moss

Introduction

This paper has emerged as part of a long-standing effort to use economic analysis to support strategic decision-making within a major multinational firm. In particular, the paper explains why and how we are exploring AI as an alternative to more orthodox game theoretic techniques.

Orthodox theory provides a very strong base for the analysis of business issues, so it is necessary to explain why it doesn't take us as far as we sometimes want to go. We do this in the next section. We then go on to explain our experiences to date with the alternative of expert systems and the current direction of our work.

Orthodox Theory: The Limitations

One of the great frustrations of traditional oligopoly theory is that, even with simple models, anything is possible. Outcomes depend, among other things, on rivals' actions and reactions, on the current and future state of the world and on the decision variables themselves.

Thus, optimum choices depend on our conjectures about rivals and the world, and on the types of actions being considered (e.g. changing prices, investing, merging, etc).

Where conditions are smooth and well defined, business economists have felt reasonably comfortable. For example, it is fairly easy to assess the short-run effects of raising the price in a market one dominates. We can describe the state of the world quantitatively on the basis of historical evidence, i.e. market data. We know from experience the likely response of rivals, viz. usually to follow the leader.

However, such narrow and well-defined circumstances are relatively few and, in the scope of a business, relatively unimportant. Major strategic decisions that will have a long-term and substantial effect on the business are more complex. For example, decisions to challenge a key rival or enter a new market have general rather than specific precedents. Moreover, there are many action variables, and thus many possible combinations of actions to assess within a state of the world that is itself diverse and uncertain.

In an attempt to deal with such cases we have tried to apply models and principles derived from the game theory literature. The promise game theory offers is straightforward. Game theory provides a much richer approach than traditional neoclassical analysis to the complexities of competitive interaction and conjectural uncertainties. And, not insignificantly, the gaming and battlefield metaphors have a particular intuitive relevance to the business world.

Unfortunately, while game theoretic models offer, in our view, considerable promise in addressing business problems, they suffer from a number of deficiencies that limit their use in the business environment. Some of these deficiencies are common to neoclassical models; others relate to the special features of the game theoretic approach.

The Models Oversimplify the World

The models are simple in order to make them tractable and to allow general equilibrium solutions. As a result they tend to describe a rather barren world that would be unrecognizable to any businessman.

Now this is perhaps too easy a criticism, one that has traditionally been levelled at economic models of all sorts. But there are at least three reasons why it is particularly relevant here. First, while the simplification may allow an equilibrium to be found, the real world is rarely in an equilibrium state. Success in business involves adapting to, or indeed exploiting, disequilibrium.

The second point is related. The literature spends a great deal of time determining whether an equilibrium exists and, when we are lucky, what its characteristics are. While the simplifications aim towards identifying equilibrium, they largely ignore the equilibrating process. Yet, it is the analysis of this process that is often most interesting to us in business. And that analysis is likely to depend heavily on the characteristics of the real environment from which the simple game has been abstracted.

This leads to the third point. The outcomes of game theoretic models are very sensitive to the information restrictions imposed. As we enrich these models with more 'realistic' assumptions, the outcomes change. The models then do not meet the standards of reliability that a business client is likely to expect.

The Models Tell What Can Happen

As Fisher (1989) has pointed out, these models tend to reflect exemplifying rather than generalizable theory. Even if we could define the environment acceptably, the models are likely to tell us what can happen, not what will. This poses obvious problems for a decision-maker, and for the economist using such models to offer advice. There are no clear lessons from the theory. The ability of economics as a positive science to tell us what will happen becomes very limited. In the worst case the results of particular versions of the models become a tool to reinforce subjective judgements.

The Models Adopt a Rigid View of Rationality

Game theoretic models implicitly assume that the players are rational. On the surface this is rather unobjectionable. Irrationality is difficult to analyse.

But the models' view of rationality is very narrow. For one thing it relies on the players processing a very restricted, and incomplete, set of information. And, as one tries to expand the information-processing requirements, one risks encountering bounded rationality.

Perhaps a more important criticism of the rationality assumptions derives from the observation of how business decisions are made. The process varies from organization to organization, but invariably involves a mix of people with complicated and sometimes conflicting motives. What is rational for an organization is difficult to define precisely.

One classical example of this lies in the challenges to profit-maximization theory. What is relevant here is less the concern about what is maximised than about the process. Rational members of a rational organization may have individual goals that are inconsistent. Brand managers, for example, compete for scarce resources to make their brands as successful as possible. Managers look for individual successes that will bring promotion to limited senior posts. Moreover, rationality doesn't require optimization. The benchmark for behaviour is more likely to be a rival than some absolute unobservable standard.

Finally, one observes that business organizations do make bad - if not necessarily irrational - decisions. Game theory does not cope well with such circumstances. Yet business judgement occasionally and legitimately involves exploiting the mistakes, the bad plays, systematic or unsystematic, of competitors.

The Models Don't Adequately Take Account of Uncertainty

In the real world, uncertain and unforeseen events can dominate outcomes. Political revolutions, product innovations, and competitive entry can change the rules of a business game. Often decisions on how to deal with such possibilities are based on business intuition.

The models' information restrictions, in a complex world, and their search for general equilibrium solutions, in a changing world, greatly lessen their relevance.   Overall, our experiences in trying to apply game theory have offered us only limited satisfaction. Theory, in the form of equilibrium solutions, provides some useful general principles, but not an active on-line decision support tool.

Perhaps an example will help to illustrate the point. Let's consider the sort of issue where game theoretic analysis would appear likely to be of considerable use. Suppose a company is considering whether to enter a new geographic market. This new market is dominated by a local firm who has long sensed the company's interest and can be presumed to have thought about its potential response.

For the potential entrant, the decision to enter will hinge on a variety of factors. A key concern is the likely reaction of the local rival. Accommodation into the oligopoly is the preferred reaction, of course. But what can it really expect? More to the point, what can game theory tell us that would be useful to the decision-maker? One proposition does stand out. The entrant needs to make a credible commitment.

This is a basic lesson from the strategy of conflict literature, but, to be generous, it can also be attributed to game theory. If the company does enter it needs to signal that it is committed. This could come from announcements, capital investment, or whatever.

But how much further can one go? Does game theory tell the potential entrant, for example, whether entry will be accommodated? Many single models suggest so, since accommodation appears the profit-optimizing strategy under single conditions. These more complex models may point out the incumbent's possible interest in signalling determination to fight and in discouraging future entrants. Empirical observation tells us that the situation is often somewhere in between: initial reactions and then accommodation.

All this is of some interest to the decision-maker, but it doesn't really address his specific decision-making problem. The strategic questions are ultimately left unanswered. If he chooses to enter, he needs to decide, the best way to achieve accommodation. What specifically does accommodation mean? At what point will it occur - what share, what time, what investment?

The decision-maker also needs to consider reactions. They can come in various forms. What will they be?
- increases in marketing,
- lowering price,
- introducing a technologically advanced product,
- retaliation in another market?

The potential entrant's reaction in turn to these - or even its presumption of reactions - will in turn provoke other reactions, and so on. We would suggest that game theory cannot handle this problem in its full complexity. There are too many variables to consider. Even more importantly, the process is dynamic and reactive and is fundamentally incapable of being dealt with by equilibrium models. What then is the alternative? For many businesses it is pure intuition. But we would like to think we can do better, at the very least informing that intuition. What we need to do is combine the general principles of economic theory with a detailed and specific knowledge of ourselves, our competitors and our markets. The result we envision is not deterministic, but is rather a set of possibilities to present to decision-makers in order to enrich their perspective. This vision led us to consider AI approaches.

What Kind of AI?

A clear advantage of expert systems for companies is that they enable us to tailor decision-making aids to the company's own circumstances. We do not need a generalized theory; we need a company-specific theory.

Note that the characteristics of a theory which is appropriate to the needs of the individual firm are not those which academic economists require. In particular, in a world which is typically in disequilibrium, we are not particularly anxious to build models with globally (much less locally) stable Nash equilibrium properties.

What we do need is a general statement of rivals' behaviour and a model of the market within which to analyse that behaviour. In this way we can run scenarios to explore a variety of strategic approaches, and to analyse those approaches on the basis of simulation set-ups reflecting our own views of the functioning of the markets in which we trade, of our rivals' decision-making procedures and our customers' behaviour.

Our first attempts at creating computer-based systems for developing strategic scenarios were in the context of a business game. For this game, we relied entirely on expert-systems techniques which, while they had some strengths relative to the game theoretic models we have challenged, turned out to have many similar limitations as well.

The game was between a team of managers and the computer. The computer as a game-player was defined by a set of expert system-type rules. These rules specify a set of conditions and

actions. If the conditions are satisfied by the current and, perhaps some past, states of the world, then the actions are taken. Our problem was to write rules which could recognize patterns of behaviour by the players of the game.
Were they being aggressive? Or passive? Were they trying to take a price-leadership role or were they price followers in some complex way? Where we had defined patterns of behaviour that matched any of these or a number of other 'personality traits', then the computer's rulebase indicated action which we had previously considered likely to be appropriate and effective.

The model had three firms, each of which had as decision variables-price, capacity and expenditure on product innovation. In addition, the players of the game and the main computer-player had to determine expenditures on marketing, product development (i.e. changing the characteristics of existing products) and process innovation. Since each firm could have any number of products, the number of decision variables times the number of firms in the model was at least fifteen and increased by six with every new product. In most games there were about six products, and so in excess of 36 strategic variables for all products and firms together.

We played this first version of the game with several large groups of managers, usually as part of a management course. They typically operated in teams of 3-5 players versus the computer. The games generally lasted about 50 rounds, although players were not told when the game would end.
We have not done a systematic analysis of the results, but three general points about the experiences are worth noting. They are interesting as an indication both of AI's limitations and its possible strengths.

'The Real World'

In comparison to theoretical repeated games models, our game could not be called simple. Yet when asked to suggest improvements to the game, the managers who had played invariably recommended additional complications to make the game more 'realistic'. The specific form of the suggestions varied and spanned issues from R&D, to marketing, to capital investment, to new entry, etc. Clearly the managers were trying to relate the game to their real world, and it was a complicated one.

Thus, we immediately came upon a problem common to game theory and A.I. Our response has been similar to the theoreticians'. We are adding more realistic assumptions subject to the constraints of tractability. All we can argue is that the AI approaches reach their limits well beyond the reality confines of theoretical models.

Criteria for Success

To make the game interesting to the management players, we have generally had the players compete. This required some criteria for success. Our discussion of the criteria raised some issues that help distinguish the orthodox and AI approaches.

When we first played the game, we suggested that the winning team should be the one with the highest profit, regardless of how the computer opponent fared. There was objection to this on two counts. One was the focus on profits rather than some other variable. The other was on the profit standard.

The alternatives to the profit variable were those that reflected the managers' own perceived criteria for reward. There were suggestions, for example, that we consider objective functions that included market share or return on capital. Such concerns pose an equal but certainly manageable challenge to both orthodox theory and AI approaches.

The more interesting objection in our view was about profit standards. Every one of the groups who played the game raised the suggestion that we judge profits relative to the computer competitor. Winning for them was about beating the competitor rather than getting close to some global maximum figure.

In discussion, this relative standard, this using of the competitor as benchmark, was defended as the only way to operate in an uncertain world. The real business environment does not give a clear view of all possible worlds. If it did, profit maximization in its purest form would have clear relevance. But our players, in relating the game to their own environment, clearly could not imagine all possible worlds. AI comes into its own in this situation. It is not constrained by a lack of knowledge of possible outcomes, nor by any need to equate rational behaviour with maximizing behaviour.

Rules of Engagement

Our game is based on a team playing against a programmed computer character. This contrasts, of course, with the more common management games between two groups of human players. Our objective has been to control the character of the computer player and by so doing to gain experience and insight about how to deal with such a competitor.

The problem arises in specifying the rules governing the computer's actions. The environment, even in its simple form, involves many variables. The human team's range of actions are many and can vary infinitely. How will - how should - the computer react? As it develops, our rules very often produced puzzling outcomes. Some of these proved insightful. Others seemed due to an inability to specify all the contingencies adequately. Indeed, we determined that we should have had to have written certainly hundreds and possibly thousands of rules to capture the main strategic modes of various teams of managers playing the game. This limits AI's ease of application, but in our view not its inherent feasibility.

There are two approaches to the problem. One is the familiar path of 'brute force'. In this context it would require a belief in a view (e.g. see Moravec (1989)) that we can in principle download our corporate consciousness into a set of specific rules that would govern every eventuality. This seemed to us less productive than a second alternative, relying on techniques of machine-learning.

With such programs we specify for each firm a (usually but not necessarily) mathematical model of the environment and a set of rules which do nothing but create the sort of action rules that we wrote for the previous versions. That is, we try to describe decision-making procedures as rules which themselves identify and implement successful behaviour in a wide variety of circumstances. In this way, we devise a relatively small set of 'meta-rules' which then 'write' action rules to set the values of decision variables. The set of action rules can be arbitrarily large and complex, though a good set of meta-rules will minimize the size and complexity of the action rulebase without loss of effectiveness.

This gives us a system for which the strategic analyst can specify his own firm's learning behaviour and decision-making procedures, rivals' learning and decision-making procedures and the characteristics of the markets in which they all compete. Nonsense results will indicate that something has been misspecified and will require the users of these systems to consider in detail how they think their markets work, how they behave and how their rivals behave. Remember that the purpose of our approach to modelling decision-making behaviour is to increase our own and managers' understandings of their environments and the effects of their actions and the actions of their competitors. Our current view is that our modelling systems should allow each simulated firm to be controlled either by the human users, or by an action rulebase or by a meta-rulebase. When the users control one or more of the competing firms, they continually assess whether the model environment is plausible and the ways in which outcomes contradict experience. Once the environment seems correctly specified, then users playing against action rulebases enable the users continually to refine their specifications of their competitors' behaviour or, if they are representing their competitors, to develop rulebases describing their own competitive behaviour.

The purpose of the meta-rulebase is to model strategic decision-making behaviour. The concerns include the identification of problems and opportunities, responses to competitors' mistakes, recovery from one's own mistakes - indeed all of the disequilibrium phenomena discussed above. It is the development of meta-rulebases which seems to us to be the most interesting and important aspect of these developments. With them, we hope to be able not only to describe strategic behaviour, but also to analyse the strengths and weaknesses of different approaches to strategic decision-making.

Conclusions

We are now in a position where we have special theories of decision-making in conditions of oligopoly embodied in artificially intelligent models. We expect more general theory to arise naturally from them.

How does this position compare with that of mainstream oligopoly theory? It seems to us that a reasonable defence of the repeated-game theories would be that they, too, are applicable in special cases, and that some general principles of use to oligopolistic firms or government regulators have arisen from them. Our principal concern would be that

results are very small relative to the effort expended. In our view, this reflects an inappropriate concentration on dubious theoretical issues at the expense of business-relevant ones. For example, it does not seem very helpful to us to claim that there are general conditions (if there are) in which oligopoly markets converge towards Nash equilibria unless we can identify cases in which actual markets do so.

6. Experiments, Games and Economics

John D. Hey[1] and Martin L. Reynolds

Introduction

Much of modern economics, particularly modern industrial organization theory, is dominated by game theory. Many theorists assume that such theory is tautologically true; consequently, it is very rarely subjected to direct empirical investigation. It is the purpose of this paper to begin to rectify this situation - through an experimental investigation of a simple game theoretic model of an R&D race that is typical of the modern industrial organization literature. This investigation has two aspects - the second of which presumes a particular outcome to the first: first, we test to see whether actual behaviour coincides with that predicted by the economic theory; second, on the presumption that behaviour is not coincident, we try to discover the actual process underlying behaviour.

Our research programme raises important methodological issues: about the status of theory in economics; about the status of direct controlled experimental investigation of theory; and about the value of economic theory as a description of real-world economic behaviour. Many economists feel considerable unease about what we are doing; others feel that what we are doing is completely irrelevant to economics - some because of their views about the

[1]   John Hey acknowledges the financial assistance of the ESRC in financing this research and the assistance of a Nuffield Social Science Fellowship during the academic year 1989/90, when much of the planning of the experiment took place. John Hey also thanks his colleagues in EXEC, the Centre for Experimental Economics at the University of York, particularly Graham Loomes, Michele Bernasconi and Giacomo Pignataro, for helpful discussions. Finally, but most importantly, John Hey would like to thank Norman Spivey for providing the networked software for the experiment.

relevance of the theory, others because of their views about the validity of the theory. To a certain extent we agree: we 'should' really be doing completely different experiments. But let us come to that conclusion later in the story.

The Game to be Investigated

We investigate an R&D patent race that is typical of the genre. It is built on modern game theory, as are most models in modern industrial organization theory. The particular R&D race that we investigate is that of Fudenberg et al. (1983). It has all the hallmarks of the type: very simple structure; well-defined rules; well-defined objectives; and an extremely complex solution.

There are 2 firms/players. Both start at the same point. There is a 'winning post', a pre-specified number of steps, n, from the starting point. The race proceeds in rounds: in each round, the 2 firms independently decide and simultaneously announce whether to go 0, 1 or 2 steps in that round. Going 0 steps costs nothing; going 1 step costs c_1; going 2 steps costs c_2. Both c_1 and c_2 are known, and c_2 is more than twice c_1. This latter is the essence of the problem: it is more efficient going 1 step in each round, but then there is the danger that the other firm will get to the winning post first. The first to the winning post gets the prize, V (a known amount); if both firms reach the winning post in the same round (and cross the winning line simultaneously), then they equally share the prize.

Describing the game is simple: what is complex is the solution. Here we confine ourselves to a bald statement of its main features; details (though not complete details) can be found in Fudenberg et al. (1983).   Moreover, we restrict attention to a subset of the parameter space for which a unique symmetric Nash equilibrium exists. Elsewhere in the parameter space, multiple, asymmetric Nash equilibria exist; these create additional complexities (though whether they would be appreciated by human beings is not obvious).

The parameters of the problem are n, V, c_1 and c_2. Let us introduce a further parameter (which depends on V and c_2) which we denote by k and represents the largest even number of steps which, if covered 2 steps per round, can still lead to positive profits for both firms while sharing the prize. Optimal behaviour under the Nash equilibrium differs fundamentally depending on whether this threshold has been passed or not. Details of this Nash equilibrium are as follows:

If both firms are more than k steps from the winning post:

If the firms are tied both should play the same mixed strategy over [0, 1, 2] steps.

If one firm is ahead the one that is ahead should play 1 and the one that is behind should play 0 (that is, drop out).

If both firms are less than or equal to k steps from the winning post:

If the firms are tied both should play 2.

If one firm is ahead
by 1 step the one that is ahead should play a mixed strategy on [1, 2] and the one that is behind should play a mixed strategy on [0, 2].

If one firm is ahead
by more than 1 step the one that is ahead should play 1 and the one that is behind should play 0 (drop out).

If one firm has more than k steps to go and the other has k or less:

The leader should play 1 and the follower play 0.

The probabilities specifying the mixed strategies are functions of V, c_1, c_2 and the number of steps remaining to the winning post. Their calculation proceeds in the usual manner, by backward induction. (Though the first-named author admits, with appropriate shame, that it took him many hours to write down the appropriate recursive formulae in a form suitable for specifying in a computer program.)

The Experimental Implementation at York

We have programmed this R&D race as a networked experiment: our software enables up to 16 subjects to play a sequence of such races against varying opponents. At any stage, a subject's opponent could be one of the other subjects or the computer, programmed to play the Nash equilibrium strategy. At York, we ran a series of 10 sessions, each involving up to 10 subjects each playing a sequence of 9 races. The same 9 races were used in each of the 10 sessions, with the order of the races varying randomly from session to session. We told the subjects that, in each race, they were racing against one of the other subjects in the room - but they were not told which. They were also told that they had a different rival in each race.   In fact, they sometimes were playing the computer.   In retrospect, it seems that this 'deception' was pointless - we shall avoid it in future experiments.   At Nottingham a different experimental procedure was invoked; we describe that later. In this section, we confine our discussion to the York experiment.

Although 10 subjects, plus 2 reserves, were booked into each of the 10 sessions, some of the sessions had to be run with less than 10 subjects since less than 10 turned up. As a consequence, the total number of subjects participating in these experiments was not 100, but 95. Furthermore, in not all of the 10 sessions were all 9 races completed, since on 2 occasions the software crashed. Nevertheless, we have a large volume of data, covering 463 races, 269 of which involved 2 human subjects and 194 of which involved one human subject playing the computer. We paid out a total of some £600; our thanks to the ESRC for financing these experiments.

The next issue to be addressed is that of analysing the data and beginning to answer the question: was actual behaviour coincident with the optimal strategy? We do not intend to answer the question fully here; this will be done elsewhere.   What we will do is to indicate that the answer is not as easy as it might appear. This is primarily because the optimal (Nash equilibrium) strategy is a mixed one.

Consider first the question of whether actual behaviour is (not in-) consistent with the optimal strategy. If the optimal strategy requires a mixed response on [0, 1, 2], then any decision is consistent with the optimal strategy; if the optimal is a mixture on [1, 2] then either 1 or 2 is consistent with the optimal; and so on. So this test is a weakish one. In Table 1 we summarize the results of this test. Overall, out of 6994 decisions made by the human subjects, 5851 (83.7 per cent) were consistent with the optimal strategy. (Of course, the computer was 100 per cent consistent.) This may appear surprisingly high, but the caveats above should be noted. Table 1 reveals that consistency (with the Nash equilibrium strategy) is higher for some races than others. In particular, races A and B have consistency rates over 90 per cent (91.1 per cent and 93.5 per cent respectively). But these 2 races are different from the other 7, in that the k in races A and B is greater than the corresponding n, so that both players could play 2 in each round and both make positive net profits. Many subjects realized this and played accordingly.

In races C through I, such a strategy was not possible, since in each of them k was less than n. This means that the expected net winnings, for each of the 2 players when both playing the Nash equilibrium, in races C through I, was zero: all the available prize money would be competed away. In contrast, the expected net winnings in races A and B were positive - equal to $V/2 - (n/2) c_2$ (199 pence and 210 pence respectively).

How close subjects came to these expected net winnings is revealed in Table 2. In races A and B, average net winnings, at 179 and 200, were marginally lower than the expected net winnings under the Nash equilibrium strategy; generally speaking this was also the case with the other 7 races, though experience varied slightly: for example, in race F, subjects did rather better than under the Nash equilibrium, while in race H, they did rather worse. It will be of interest to check whether the results in Tables 1 and 2 shed any light on the question of whether behaviour (relative to the Nash equilibrium) was influenced by the parameters.

Of course, the Nash equilibrium is not necessarily a model for behaviour. Consider, for example, race C. In this, the expected net winnings for each player under the Nash equilibrium is zero. If,

Table 6.1   Parameters and simple consistency checks

Race letter	Prize V (pence)	Steps n	Costs c_1	Costs c_2 pence	Against other subjects c	Against other subjects t	Against other subjects p	Against the computer c	Against the computer t	Against the computer p	Totals c	Totals t	Totals p
A	518	20	2	6	583	646	.902	252	271	.930	835	917	.911
B	520	10	2	10	286	308	.929	115	121	.950	401	429	.935
C	186	5	2	46	170	196	.867	60	67	.896	230	263	.875
D	258	10	8	32	303	350	.866	135	152	.888	438	502	.873
E	206	10	4	34	302	379	.797	111	125	.888	413	504	.819
F	262	15	4	26	479	626	.765	201	243	.827	680	869	.783
G	274	15	6	34	455	564	.807	205	237	.865	660	801	.824
H	422	20	10	42	780	974	.801	204	252	.810	984	1226	.803
I	442	25	10	22	925	1140	.811	285	343	.831	1210	1483	.816
TOTALS					4283	5183	.826	1568	1811	.866	5851	6994	.837

Key:

c: number of decisions consistent with Nash equilibrium strategy

t: total number of decisions

p: ratio of c to t - proportion of steps consistent with the NE

Table 6.2   Average net winnings by race letter and number

Race	1	2	3	4	5	6	7	8	9	All Letter
A	159	199	199	164	199		173		206	179
B	165			196	210	210	212	187		200
C	-16	16	1						4	2
D	-11	-16	-8	-12				11	11	-1
E	-10	39		7	6		-20	-14		-4
F		-17		17	15	22				11
G	36	-40	8		-59	-27			12	-22
H	158	-48	-121	-83		61		-37		-71
I	-39	32				-8	-40	-11	5	-5
All	30	18	-6	66	35	35	87	14	34	34

Notes:

(1)   All averages are the appropriately weighted averages

(2)   Empty cells indicate no observations

(3)   In full cells numbers of observations vary from cell to cell

however, both players go 1 step each round, they would share the prize at a cost of just 10 pence each - so they would each get net winnings of 83 pence. (Even better is for one player to play 0, the other to play 1, and then for them to share the prize.) Inspection of the results of the experiment suggests that some players were indeed trying to reach such an outcome - but, in the absence of communication, it is difficult to achieve.

Given that the Nash equilibrium strategy is partly of a mixed form, a more appropriate test of the consistency of actual behaviour with the optimal is provided by a comparison of the observed relative frequencies of certain decisions with the theoretically-derived probabilities for those decisions. Tables 3 and 4 provide such a comparison for races C and E. From Table 3, for example, it can be seen that subjects, when tied with their rivals with less than (k + 1) steps to go, played 1 (and indeed 0) some of the time, even though they should have played 2 all the time. It is not quite clear why they did this - unless the arguments of the paragraph above are relevant. Two things that quite clearly emerge from Tables 3 and 4 are that subjects kept going for too long (playing 1 and 2 when they 'should' have played 0), and that they kept on playing 2 when sufficiently far ahead for them to drop to 1. This may be due to risk-aversion. It may, however, be due to them playing strategies other than the Nash equilibrium. Of course, if they detected that their opponent was not playing the Nash equilibrium, then it is perfectly rational for them not to do so.

Such issues are the concern of the next section.

The Experimental Implementation at Nottingham

The experimental implementation of the R&D race at Nottingham was similar to that at York and involved using identical software. Subjects each played a sequence of 9 races. The significant difference between the York and Nottingham experiments was in terms of the approach to data collection. In the remainder of this paper we shall outline an approach to studying the actual processes underlying subject behaviour in the R&D race.

In the previous section we described the characteristics of the

Player's relative position	k	No. of obs.	0 steps taken			1 step taken			2 steps taken		
			a	b	c	a	b	c	a	b	c
Player more than 1 step behind rival	1	0	-	-	1	-	-	0	0	-	0
	2	0	-	-	1	-	.17	0	0	-	0
	3	6	5	.83	1	1	.33	0	0	0	0
	4*	3	2	.67	1	1	.33	0	0	0	0
	5	6	4	.67	1	2		0	0	0	0
Player exactly 1 step behind rival	1	0	-	-	-	-	-	0	-	-	0
	2	10	1	.10	.5629	0	0	0	9	.90	.4731
	3	5	1	.20	.6934	2	.40	0	2	.40	.3066
	4*	14	1	.07	.5835	6	.43	0	7	.50	.4615
	5	0	-	-	1	-	-	0	-	-	0
Player tied with rival	1	35	0	0	0	9	.26	0	26	.74	1
	2	6	0	0	0	2	.33	0	4	.67	1
	3	38	1	.03	0	5	.13	0	32	.84	1
	4*	6	0	0	0	6	1	0	0	0	1
	5	81	3	.04	.0091	20	.25	.3716	58	.72	.6193
Player exactly 1 step ahead of rival	1	10	0	0	0	3	.30	.4946	7	.70	.5054
	2	3	0	0	0	3	1	.9787	0	0	.0213
	3	22	0	0	0	6	.27	.9787	16	.73	.0213
	4*	0	-	-	0	-	-	1	-	-	0
	5	0	-	-	0	-	-	1	-	-	0
Player more than 1 step ahead of rival	1	13	0	0	0	13	1	1	0	0	0
	2	3	0	0	0	3	1	1	0	0	0
	3	2	0	0	0	2	1	1	0	0	0
	4*	0	-	-	0	-	-	1	-	-	0
	5	0	-	-	0	-	-	1	-	-	0

k: number of steps left to winning post for player
a: frequency
b: relative frequency
c: probability

Table 6.4 Probability and frequency distributions: race E

Player's relative position	k	No. of obs.	0 steps taken a	0 steps taken b	0 steps taken c	1 step taken a	1 step taken b	1 step taken c	2 steps taken a	2 steps taken b	2 steps taken c
Player more than 1 step behind rival	1	0	-	-	-	-	-	-	-	-	0
	2	0	-	-	1	-	-	0	-	-	0
	3	3	2	.67	1	1	.33	0	0	0	0
	4	7	5	.71	1	1	.14	0	1	.14	0
	5	2	0	0	1	2	1	0	0	0	0
	6*	8	6	.75	1	2	.25	0	0	.06	0
	7	17	15	.88	1	1	.06	0	1	.06	0
	8	14	8	.57	1	3	.21	0	3	.21	0
	9	22	21	.95	1	1	.05	0	0	0	0
	10	9	8	.89	1	1	.11	0	0	0	0
Player exactly 1 step behind rival	1	0	-	-	1	-	-	0	-	-	0
	2	6	1	.17	.7087	0	0	0	5	.83	.2913
	3	2	0	0	.8045	0	0	0	2	1	.1955
	4	5	0	0	.7374	1	.20	0	4	.80	.2626
	5	6	0	0	.8045	3	.50	0	3	.50	.1955
	6*	2	0	0	.7853	0	0	0	2	1	.2147
	7	8	3	.38	1	2	.25	0	3	.38	0
	8	2	0	0	1	2	1	0	0	0	0
	9	15	3	.20	1	6	.40	0	0	.40	0
	10	1	0	0	1	0	0	0	1	1	0

90

Player tied with rival

k	a	b	c	a	b	c	a	b	c
1	0	0	0	0	0	0	1	1	1
2	0	0	0	0	0	0	26	1	1
3	1	.14	0	4	.57	0	2	.29	1
4	0	0	0	4	.15	0	23	.85	1
5	0	0	0	7	.70	0	3	.30	1
6*	0	0	0	8	.27	0	22	.73	1
7	0	0	.0209	5	.71	.1920	2	.29	.7871
8	1	.02	.0225	8	.19	.1598	33	.79	.8177
9	0	0	.0230	6	1	.1680	0	0	.8090
10	3	.04	.0235	23	.31	.1719	49	.65	.8046

Player exactly 1 step ahead of rival

k	a	b	c	a	b	c	a	b	c
1	0	0	0	3	.75	.3301	1	.25	.6699
2	0	0	0	0	0	.4928	2	1	.5072
3	0	0	0	0	0	.4928	3	1	.5072
4	0	0	0	0	0	.9714	3	1	.0286
5	0	0	0	0	0	.9714	2	1	.0286
6*	0	0	0	3	.30	1	7	.70	0
7	0	0	0	2	1	1	0	0	0
8	1	.08	0	4	.31	1	8	.62	0
9	0	0	0	1	.50	1	1	.50	0
10	0	0	—	0	0	—	0	0	—

Player more than 1 step ahead of rival

k	a	b	c	a	b	c	a	b	c
1	4	.17	0	19	.83	1	0	0	0
2	1	.05	0	19	.95	1	0	0	0
3	0	0	0	16	1	1	0	0	0
4	0	0	0	15	.88	1	2	.12	0
5	0	0	0	11	.92	1	1	.08	0
6*	0	0	0	13	.93	1	1	.07	0
7	0	0	0	6	1	1	0	0	0
8	0	0	0	2	1	1	0	0	0
9	0	0	0	0	—	1	0	0	0
10	0	0	0	0	—	1	0	0	0

k: number of steps left to winning post for player
a: frequency
b: relative frequency
c: probability

optimal (Nash equilibrium) strategy; for example it was noted that the optimal strategy was primarily a mixed one (ie decisions 0, 1 or 2).

It is useful to distinguish between the optimal strategy in terms of decision outcome and decision process (following Simon's concepts of substantive and procedural rationality).   Pursuing a strategy implies deliberation and planning of action. In the context of the R&D race it is clearly possible for a subject to make an optimal decision without necessarily pursuing the optimal strategy (as discussed earlier). Hence, the caveats that need to be placed on the behavioural interpretation of the results stated earlier. We have seen that the optimal strategy fundamentally depends upon the values of the race parameters and, in particular, the value for k. While the decision choices facing subjects in the experiment are simple (move 0, 1 or 2 steps), the reasoning behind the optimal move is more complex to understand.   Despite the high level of consistency between the actual decisions made by the subjects at York and the optimal decision (see Table 1), is it possible to infer whether subjects were pursuing the optimal strategy in the terms described earlier?

The previous comments are likely to take on greater significance for decision problems that are complex and ill-defined, and where it may not even be possible to define an optimal solution. However, even within the very simple structure of our R&D experiment, the analysis of the results suggests that it would be helpful to consider more than just decision output data for assessing the extent to which actual decisions are coincident with the optimal choices predicted by economic theory.

Verbal Protocol Analysis

The discussion above suggests the need for an approach to the collection of data that aids the understanding of the actual decision-making processes that characterize behaviour. For this purpose the Nottingham experiments used the technique of verbal protocol analysis. This involved asking subjects to 'think aloud' during the experiment. Verbal protocol analysis is one example of a range of process-tracing techniques that are concerned with identifying the information-processing regularities in decision-making behaviour.

Verbal protocol data can either be collected concurrently during the actual performance of a task (e.g. Newell and Simon (1972)) or retrospectively after the task has been completed (e.g. Nisbett and Wilson (1977)).

Protocol analysis is generally acknowledged as a resource-intensive and time-consuming activity. However, it is arguably the best available technique for making a detailed observation and study of human decision processes. For the purpose of the analysis outlined below, we shall use the protocol of a single subject. Further analysis of the protocols of other subjects who participated in the experiments at Nottingham is required before we can assess the general validity of any conclusions.

Our approach to the use of protocol analysis is closely linked with Newell and Simon's theory of human problem-solving. Problem-solving is viewed as a path - a series of inter-connected knowledge states - through a problem space. A problem space is defined as the subject's internal representation of a particular task. One output of protocol analysis is the specification of a subject's problem space.

Protocol analysis can be used in a number of different ways. For example, scanning the protocol for simple anecdotal evidence; scoring the frequency of use of certain types of information or activities; global modelling of the decision-making process; simulation modelling of decision processes. In the analysis below we focus on the global modelling of behaviour with the purpose of putting some initial structure to the knowledge state sequences that characterise our subject's behaviour during the running of the experiment. From this we can begin to develop an understanding of the decision-making strategies used by the subject.

In essence, protocol analysis involves looking for regularity and patterns in a subject's verbal comments (these regular patterns help define the heuristic decision rules used by a subject). If each problem situation involved the subject using a unique process it would not be possible to verify a model of the subject's behaviour. A useful initial step is to break the transcribed protocol into 'thought units' or 'topic elements' - discrete steps that represent a single idea or activity of a subject during decision-making. Once the protocol has been broken up into thought units it is then possible to code each topic statement in terms of the elements that make up the subject's perceived problem space.

The problem space defines the knowledge elements and operators that reflect a subject's perception of a particular task. Knowledge elements simply represent some state of knowledge in the problem space, and state what the subject can know in performing a task. Operators correspond closely to information-processing activities. Operators take existing states of knowledge as inputs and produce new states of knowledge as output.

A Protocol Analysis of Subject Behaviour: Some Preliminary Findings From the Nottingham Experiments

Appendix I contains the transcribed protocol for Subject 1 (S1). S1 was an academic member of staff at Nottingham Business School. The protocol has been broken down into 'thought units' which represent the subject dealing with a single piece of information or a single activity.

Each thought unit in S1's protocol has been assigned an operator code. The operators have been identified by logging the repetitive occurrence of particular decision processes and the information elements that form the input and output of these processes. This does not imply that a single information process is associated with a particular operator; indeed, the operational specification of an operator for computer modelling (simulation) purposes may require a set of production rules for representing sub-processes (Newell and Simon (1972)). See, for example, the FS operator described below.

The previous comment suggests that decision-making can be viewed as taking place not just in one problem space, but in a hierarchy of problem spaces - the lower order spaces representing information processes that more closely correspond to the elementary information processes (EIPs) that are generic to all human problem-solving behaviour. These EIPs in turn form the basis for defining more macroscopic operators. Too high a level of aggregation is likely to be problematic for the purpose of developing behavioural process models ie. the process 'disappears'. However, protocol analysis that is too disaggregated also has its problems. There is the danger of detailing sub-processes that are not problematic for the subject, and as such do not add anything to our understanding of the subject's behaviour. Selecting the 'right' level of problem space specification is a difficult issue.

The thought unit or topic element representation of S1's protocol provides insight into some important characteristics of the subject's behaviour:

(i) S1 regularly reviews the race data and makes some attempt to interpret its significance. For example, S1 appears to develop a heuristic for assessing whether a particular race is 'worthwhile' entering. This heuristic was explicitly applied in the majority of the 9 races for which his behaviour was observed. It is a heuristic that suggests the use of a parameter similar to the k variable described earlier.

(ii) A number of statements in the subject's protocol suggest that he develops strategies during the running of the experiment (relating to the experiment, an individual race and an individual round). These strategies are influenced by a number of factors, eg. the rival's behaviour, the relative values for the step costs and prize in a race, and the stage of the race.

It is worth pointing out that in running the experiment at Nottingham we observed a tendency towards 'active participation' in all races - even where this might conflict with a strategy for the experiment in general. S1 provides examples of this.

(iii) The subject does review his decisions and those of the rival with a view to re-examining his strategies and the significance of any changes in the race data.

The protocol for S1 contains 'gaps' in the description of what the subject is doing. For example, in race 4 and race 5 the subject does not verbalize fully all the decisions that he takes (see, for example, topic statements 42 and 46). However, in most instances where gaps do exist in the protocol it is usually clear what the subject is doing, and there are only a few examples of where idiosyncrasies creep into his behaviour (see, for example, race 8 - topic statement 65).

In general, we can make some interesting observations about the process characteristics of S1's behaviour from his verbal protocol transcript. A number of these observations provide additional insight to subject behaviour to that provided by the analysis in Section 3:

(a) A 'Successful' Strategy for the Experiment

S1 articulates a sensible strategy for achieving positive winnings (though not maximizing), and minimizing the chance of sustaining losses. This is not a strategy that appears to have been pursued throughout the 9 races, but one that evolves from the subject's interpretation of the gaming situation in the experiment. In race 6, topic statement 48, the subject makes a clear statement of what he thinks is the best strategy to pursue - 'play those races where you can take positive winnings, irrespective of the cost of making 2 steps and/or the decisions of the competitor, and do not play any other races'. Races 2, 5, 6 and 7 are good examples of where this strategy is applied successfully. Indeed, if the subject had followed this strategy for all his 9 races his total net winnings would have been greater than what he actually achieved.

The comments in the protocol suggest that S1 is employing a similar variable to the k parameter identified earlier. This would tend to support the view found in the York experiments that where k is greater than n, subjects were able to articulate and follow the Nash equilibrium strategy. What is less clear for S1 is why he failed to follow this strategy throughout the experiment.

(b) A Strategy for Entering a Race

The subject makes reference to explicit criteria he applies for his decision to enter a race. For example, in race 3 (topic statement 27) and race 4 (topic statement 38), the subject's comments indicate an activity where he is making a calculation to estimate the potential net benefits of entering a race. This calculation involves comparing the cost of moving to the winning post (assuming two-step movements) against the value of the prize, assuming the subject and the rival share the prize. Once again this reinforces the suggestion that our subject was employing a k type variable based on V and c_2.

The protocol transcript indicates that S1 does not always follow this strategy. For example, in race 9 the subject has applied the heuristic for assessing whether he should enter the race, and despite noting that the race 'isn't worth winning' (topic statement 81), he enters the race. Similarly, the strategic focus in race 4 is also blurred and this would also appear to be a race that he should not have entered given his well-articulated strategy for determining whether a race is worthwhile.

The latter comments are important. They suggest a number of possibilities. Subjects may not be able to articulate the optimal decision in races where k was less than n. In these circumstances the decisions of the rival become important. For example, S1's protocol provides insight into some attempt to 'out-guess' the competitor. There are also suggestions that S1 was prepared to compete away the prize money at the expense of his own aggregate net winnings.

(c) S1's Strategy Within A Race

S1's protocol transcript reveals a number of different strategies that appear to characterize his behaviour during a race (some of these are clearly non-optimal). However, it is not always clear from the protocol as to the trigger mechanisms for a particular strategy, and S1 does not articulate any conflict resolution strategies that may have been implicit in his behaviour. Indeed, it may be that some strategies were idiosyncratic; see, for example, the strategy for race 8 (eg. comments in topic statements 65 and 71).

S1's inter-race strategy is not always revealed within the protocol. For example, there is clear evidence from the decision output data that S1 recognizes the opportunity cost associated with exiting a race where net winnings are going to be negative if the prize is shared. There is no indication of any formal calculations being applied, but there are comments that suggest he appreciates the problems of 'catching-up' with a rival (see for example topic statement 18 in race 1). Similarly, it appears that his actions imply recognition of a cut-off point beyond which the net losses of exiting a race exceed the net losses of continuing to compete in the race and sharing the prize. Once again, there is no indication from the protocol that a calculation of any sort is being made; however, his actions in race 3, race 4 and race 9 suggest an awareness of this cut-off point.

Finally, it is useful to comment on race 8. It is a good example of where the subject does not play the Nash equilibrium strategy. S1 was clearly changing his strategy when he entered the race in round 3. In general, S1's entry strategy had been to enter a race in round 1 and move 2 steps. In race 8, S1 had decided that the race was not worth entering (see topic statement 61). This was consistent with his stated strategy for the experiment. There is a suggestion in the protocol that S1's decision to enter race 8 was experimental and was activated by the rival making a 1-step move in round 2. In fact, S1's decision to enter race 8 proved to be successful as it was the only race where net winnings were positive, even though the race did not satisfy his 'satisficing' entry criterion.

It now remains to conclude our analysis by specifying S1's problem space. The topic representation of S1's protocol and our review of simple anecdotal evidence relating to his strategies provides us with the basic units of analysis for developing his problem space. The operator codes assigned to each topic statement in the protocol transcript are those defined in the problem space below. The problem space is shown in BNF notation, following Newell and Simon (1972). BNF is a useful form of meta-notation for describing grammars of programming languages.

Nottingham Experiments: Problem Space for Subject 1

Knowledge Elements

```
<race parameters> ::= cost_1/cost_2/steps_win/step_0/step_1/
          step_2/prize/race_round/race_number/
     net_winnings/previous_winnings/
          rival_decisions/<race result>
<values> ::= <digits>
<race  variables> ::=  <race  parameters>  <values>/<race
```

variables>
< race type > :: = high value/low value/?
< competitor strategy > :: = < race variables > /?
< race result > :: = win/lose/ < race variables > /?
< experiment strategy > :: =
increase_net_winnings/minimize_losses/?
< race strategy > :: = enter_race/exit_race/continue_race/?
< round strategy > :: = < decision > / < competitor strategy > /?
< strategy > :: = < experiment strategy > < race strategy >
            < round strategy > / < competitor strategy > /?
< decision > :: = step_0/step_1/step_2
< task variable > :: =
< assignment expression > :: =   < task variable > < -- < task
variable >   < expression > :: =   < task variable > / < assignment
expression >
< state expression > :: = < expression > / < expression >
< knowledge state > :: = < state expression > / < knowledge state >
            < state expression >
< goal > :: = get < decision >
< sub-goal > :: = get < expression > /check < expression >

Operator Elements

RRD/RV/FS/D/DR
It is not possible to prove that actual decision-making takes place in
a particular problem space. However, Newell and Simon (1972)
argue that the existence of a problem space is the major invariant of
problem-solving behaviour that holds across task domains and
subjects. This perspective is fundamental, since if we can define
an individual's problem space it should be possible to model
decision-making behaviour within a production system framework
(ie a computer simulation model). In sum, the specification of a
subject's problem space implies that we are able to construct a
model of procedural rationality for behaviour in a particular task
domain (even where a model of substantive rationality cannot be
defined). This highlights the value of protocol analysis as a
technique for studying behaviour in complex task domains.

Our brief description of each operator in S1's problem space below, together with the knowledge elements, gives an indication of how the LHS (left hand side) and RHS (right hand side) elements of production rules can be specified for the purpose of developing a computer model to simulate subject behaviour. Such a model might be tested against alternative race scenarios and used as a predictive model of subject behaviour.

RRD Operator (Review Race Data): this operator has a 'house-keeping' role and simply represents the subject reviewing the race parameters. There are many examples of the RRD operator being used by the subject (see topic statements 1, 13, 21, 26 and 37).

RV Operator (Race Value): this operator captures the information-processing activity of S1 assessing whether a particular race is worthwhile entering. We have described the nature of this process above and related it to the Nash equilibrium strategy. The inputs to this operator (see the problem space) are the < race variables >, and the output is a value for < race type >. A 'HIGH VALUE' race would be entered, while a 'LOW VALUE' race would not be entered if S1 were pursuing his loss minimization strategy.

FS Operator (Formulate Strategy): we have commented on the nature of the strategies pursued by S1. From our problem space definition we can identify knowledge elements relating to a number of aspects of S1's strategy: < experiment strategy >; < race strategy >; < round strategy > and < competitor strategy >. The importance of this operator is a reflection of the complexity of the task, and the production rules that define the operator will give some insight into the procedurally rational aspects of the subject's behaviour. For example, the production rules that define < race strategy > would specify the circumstances under which the subject will 'enter'; 'exit' or 'continue' a race (see the discussion above).

D Operator (Decision): this operator largely reflects the decision-making requirements of the experimental design ie. 0 step, 1 step or 2-step, and its knowledge element inputs are a function of the outputs from the other operators. In essence, this operator is capturing the information-processing activity underpinning the subject's decisions in each race.

DR Operator (Decision Review): this operator is evident from a number of comments in the subject's protocol (see, for example, topic statements 20, 25, 33, 36 and 43). It reflects the information-processing activity of the subject assessing and evaluating previous decisions (his own and those of the rival). The output of the operator is < race result >.

The problem space specification for S1 provides a framework for the development of a computer-based PS model to simulate his behaviour. The core of such a model is the production rules that define the problem space operators. In studying the behaviour of other subjects, it will be possible to verify the robustness of the problem space specification as a global model of subject behaviour for this experimental task. This, however, is beyond the scope of this paper.

To complete this section we shall illustrate the nature of the production rules that specify the operators defined in the problem space. For this purpose we shall focus on the RV operator as an example. To develop a computer-based simulation model of S1's behaviour would require that all operators are specified in production rule format.

To develop production rules for the RV operator we need to study the topic statement. It should be noted that the protocol does not reveal fully the exact detail of the information-processing activity associated with the RV operator. The authors have used their judgement and knowledge of the task domain to infer what this detail is likely to be.

We have seen that the RV operator represents the subject's information-processing activity of assessing whether a race is worthwhile in terms of the potential of making profit if the prize is shared with the competitor. In general terms (using the problem space notation), the RV operator can be specified as:

P(ID) get <race type>
   --> RV (<race variables>)
     (=> <race type> <-- high/low/?)

As it stands, this rule would be one of a set that captures the information-processing behaviour of the subject for the task. To operationalize this at the level of a computer simulation model, requires the specification of a subset of rules that reflects the way the RV operator was applied by S1 in particular circumstances during the exercise. This would require the authors to reflect on S1's decision-making strategies as described above.

The protocol allows a reasonable interpretation of what the subject was doing when applying the RV operator. For example, a key subset rule for the RV operator would involve the following information-processing activity:

(race_winnings)/2 - [(steps_win)/2] * cost_2

All the topic statements support this assertion. The net value of this calculation allows the subject to assign the qualitative statement that the <race type> is 'high', 'low' or '?'. The reader will note that our interpretation of S1's behaviour suggests that the subject was using a similar parameter to the 'k' variable described in Section 2.

Conclusions

This paper presents some preliminary findings from two pieces of experimental work using a simple patent race model. One aim has been to investigate the extent to which individual behaviour coincides with that predicted by economic theory (the optimal strategy). The experimental implementation at York used decision output data to test whether subjects were making decisions consistent with the Nash equilibrium strategy. At Nottingham, process data were collected using verbal protocol techniques to assess whether the process characteristics underlying subject behaviour were consistent with the optimal strategy. In both experimental settings there was evidence that some subjects were not pursuing the Nash equilibrium strategy.

Of equal importance in this paper are the methodological issues raised by the research programme used by the authors. Experimental studies of the type presented here are still relatively novel, and yet the opportunities for using experimental investigation to enhance our understanding of real-world economic behaviour are likely to be substantial. This research has used experiments to test the validity of predictions generated by economic theory. However, we have not been rigorous in our analysis of non-optimal strategies, and the second part of the paper was limited to outlining an approach to identifying how we might discover what strategies may have been used by subjects and how they might be modelled.

It might be argued that we should be doing quite different experiments - experiments that are not constrained by the reference points provided by existing models in economic theory. The domain of experimental economics has yet to be defined precisely, but the opportunity for undertaking 'discovery' research is a challenge that could substantially extend the domain of economic theory.

In sum, it is relevant to ask whether economists should be constrained to developing experimental designs for studying behaviour in only those task domains where optimal decisions are defined. It is our view that there remain many economic problems where the concepts of equilibrium and optimality have no meaningful behavioural relevance (and probably cannot be defined). In these circumstances we need a framework for discovering and analysing the effectiveness of the different strategies that describe economic behaviour. The research programme used here presents one approach to how economists might progress the study of behaviour in task domains that are characterized by uncertainty, complexity and limited information.

APPENDIX I

Nottingham Experiments: Protocol Transcript for Subject S1

Subject 1: Topic Statement and Decision Log

S = subject R = competitor

Operator		Topic Statement

Practice Race

RRD	1	.... the finish line in this race is 5 steps ... cost of taking 1 step is 2p .... and the cost of 2 ... 46 .... 186 for winning ....
RV	2	right ... the prize - 5 rounds .... eh .... with only 5 steps and 46 pence - you are only winning approximately 4 times ... ...
FS (Comp)	3	right ... ... what is he going to do?
FS (Race)	4	it is worth doing .... I think
FS (Round)	5	- worth going 1 ... worth going 1 ....
D	6	ready to make a decision - D ... ... 1 ... .
FS (Race) this ...	7	.... no ... I'm not prepared to play
D 0 ?	8	D ... how many steps do you want to play ...

DR	9	.... well we didn't do very well there .... let's see .... -2p ... ... should have put that 2 up ... but then again ... ... he ... I realized he would probably do that ... ...
FS (Exp)	10	so then it's a question of whether you are prepared to double it ... ... to get anything back or lose 2p ... or lose more - still lose out ...
FS (Exp)	11	... ... clearly, I think you've either got to brave it out ... on a low winnings race and hope that the other bloke doesn't ...
FS (Race)	12	so if it is a fairly low prize - go for the high value ... ... wait to see what happens ... or alternatively, ... think ... ...

Race 1

Race 1:	Cost of 1 Step: 2
	Cost of 2 Step: 46
	Winning Post: 5
	Prize Money: 186

RRD	13	... ... right ... step 1 ... race 1 ... 5 steps ... 2p to move 1 ... 46p to move 2 ... ... right ...
DR	14	Round 1 ... I've done 2 steps and he did 1 ...
FS (Comp)	15	... this time I think ... either ... he won't go any more because he has only done 1 step and the cost is greater ...

D	16	so this time we'll go 1 step ...
DR	17	... ... he's gone 2 ... ...
FS (Round)	18	this time I'm going to have to go for 2 steps again ... ... because if I go 1 and he goes 2 - the cost of catching up ... is going to be even greater ...
D	19	so 2 steps - decision 2 ....
DR	20	mmm .... didn't have any option there ... ...

Race Number 1:

Round 1 2 3
S's decision 2 1 2
R's decision 1 2 2
Net winnings: -1

Race 2

Race 2:	Cost of 1 Step: 2
	Cost of 2 Step: 6
	Winning Post: 20
	Prize Money: 518

RRD	21	... 20 steps ... ... phew! ... 20 steps ... 518p ...
FS (Race)	22	clearly, this with the low rate ... and the high number of steps ... all you just simply have to do is take 2 steps at every go ...

RV	23	... but will you make any money? ... 2 steps ... 6p ... that's 120p - a cost of 120p ... ... yes you get more back with even half of the winning prize than you would by not competing or anything ...

FS (Round)	24	so ... I think we are going to have to go 2 steps ... ... I think this is just a question of doing 2 steps ... ...

DR	25	.... didn't have any option there ... with a low cost and a high prize ... everybody was going to do that .... so that was pretty clear cut ... let's see what the next one is ... .

Race Number 2:

Round 1 2 3 4 5 6 7 8 9 10
S's decision 2 2 2 2 2 2 2 2 2 2
R's decision 2 2 2 2 2 2 2 2 2 2
Net winnings: 199

Race 3

Race 3:		Cost of 1 Step: 6 Cost of 2 Step: 34 Winning Post: 15 Prize Money: 274

RRD	26	... ... Race 3 ... right 15 steps ... ... 6p for 1 ... 34p for 2 and the total winnings 274p ...

RV	27	let's just make a calculation here ... so 15 steps ... ... 7 ... let's just see ... so ... 34 times ... 8 steps ... 272p ... ... er ... so

even the cost .... this is interesting .... there are clearly 15 steps at 34p ... ... this is going to be more than the prize is worth ... ... we could even lose money ...

D	28	mmm ... let's go with the 34p ...
DR	29	... ah! ... he did that as well ...
FS (Race)	30	let's bluff him ... let's go same again ... ...
RRD	31	ah! ah! ... ... 4 steps ... 11 to go ... ...
D	32	let's do it again ...
DR	33	see what he did ... ah! ... ...
D	34	... so we're half way there ... ... ah!! ... ... got to give it another 2 ...
D	35	too far ... ... got to go ... take this extra one ...
DR	36	oh! .... I'm not so happy about that ... ... mmm ... ... ah ... I just did 1 on the last round and he did 2 .... oh well ... ...

Race Number 3:

Round 1 2 3 4 5 6 7 8
S's decision 2 2 2 2 2 2 2 1
R's decision 2 2 2 2 2 2 2 2
Net winnings: -244

Race 4

Race 4:		Cost of 1 Step: 4
		Cost of 2 Step: 34
		Winning Post: 10
		Prize Money: 206

RRD	37	... ... 10 steps ... 1 step equals 4 ... 2 equals 34 ... 206p is the prize .... 10 steps
RV	38	... ... so if I were to take 10 steps ... 5 times 34 - 150p ...
FS (Race)	39	... anyway ... got to go 2 steps in the first round ...
DR	40	let's see what happens ... ... he went 2 steps as well - of course he did ...
D	41	... 2 steps again ... ... 68p ... ...
FS (Race)	42	I think I'll play this one through ... ...
DR	43	right ... so he did exactly the same ... so we'll share the prize .... ah ... ... yes ....

Race Number 4:

Round 1 2 3 4 5
S's decision 2 2 2 2
R's decision 2 2 2 2
Net winnings: -67

Race 5

Race 5:	Cost of 1 Step: 2
	Cost of 2 Step: 10
	Winning Post: 10
	Prize Money: 520

RRD	44	... 2p, 10p and 520p ...

FS (Race)	45	we've got another one of these ... where we sort of .... one of these where it is pretty obvious that ... ... everybody is going to go down the line of 10p all the time ... ...

FS (Race)	46	... ... simply playing 2s all the way and take a share of the prize money here ... ... right ....

Race Number 5:

Round 1 2 3 4 5
S's decision 2 2 2 2 2
R's decision 2 2 2 2 2
Net winnings: 210

Race 6

Race 6:	Cost of 1 Step: 4
	Cost of 2 Step: 26
	Winning Post: 15
	Prize Money: 262

RRD	47	... ... prize 15 steps

FS (Expt)	48	... I think the secret to this is that you take your winnings on the easy games and then you simply don't play on the others ... if not

..... you are likely to come off second best and hardly win anything

| RV | 49 | ... here for instance ... 15 steps ... so 8 ... 8 times 26p .... will be 208 .... so you spend 208p to get 100p or so back |

| FS (Race) | 50 | ... so again it isn't worth playing ... |

| D | 51 | so I think with this one our decision will be 0 |
... .

| FS (Race) | 52 | then we'll 0 everything else and not play ... |
... ...

| DR | 53 | right ... so we didn't play that one - so we haven't lost anything ... |
| FS (Exp) | 54 | but then again, since the idea is to build up as much as we can win - then that's not the problem ... ... 97p ... let's see what we do with the next one ... ... |

Race Number 6:

Round 1 2 3 4 5 6 7 8 91011121314
S's decision 0 0 0 0 0 0 0 0 0 0 0 0 0 0
R's decision 2 1 1 1 1 1 1 1 1 1 1 1 1 1
Net winnings: 0

Race 7

Race 7:   Cost of 1 Step: 10
            Cost of 2 Step: 22
            Winning Post: 25
            Prize Money: 442

RRD	55	... ... oh ..... a little mad with the values here ... 25 steps 420p

RV	56	... ... so that's going to be ... ... 14 times 22 ... ... equals 308p ... ... 55 ... so if we half that ....

FS (Race)	57	with a high value ... we are going to lose ... no I'm not going to play this one either ...

FS (Exp)	58	.... if we play for half the winnings of this ... ... there is going to be no real opportunity to win ... ... right ...

FS (Race)	59	... hold on though ... . no we'll stick to what we said - we won't play ... ... mmm ... ...

Race Number 7:

Round 1 2 3 4 5 6 7 8 9 10 11 12 13 14 15 16 17 18 19 20 21 22 23 24
S's decision 0 0 0 0 0 0 0 0 0 0 0 0 0 0 0 0 0 0 0 0 0 0 0 0
R's decision 2 1 1 1 1 1 1 1 1 1 1 1 1 1 1 1 1 1 1 1 1 1 1 1
Net winnings: 0

Race 8

Race 8:	Cost of 1 Step: 10
	Cost of 2 Step: 42
	Winning Post: 20
	Prize Money: 422

RRD	60	... ... 20 steps ... ...

RV	61	... ... clearly, ... what you should do I suppose is ... you should bet .... if you look ... you divide ... ... the winning total by

half ... ... what would that be ... 261p ... ...
no ... 211p ... ... mmm ... .
no ... there isn't ... no ... if you got to the end
... ...

FS (Comp)	62	no - I don't know what he is going to do ... ... if his first move is going to be 42p ... ... then after that he'll probably go 42p ... ...
FS (Race)	63	... as long as I do 42p ... ... so ultimately you lose ... ... the money ... let's not play ... ... mmm ... ...
FS (Comp)	64	he'll go to 10p ... ...
FS (Round)	65	let's try and shake him ... let's go to 42p ... ... now ... ... that'll have put the cat amongst the ... ...
D	66	let's do 42p again ...
DR	67	ah! ... ... now ... that's interesting ... .
D	68	let's try it again - let's go for 42p again ... ...
FS (Comp)	69	he'll probably go 42p this time - he can't let me ... ...
D	70	oh! ... ... right let's drop down to 10p
FS (Exp)	71	... ... I'm not sure what my 'grand' strategy is here ... then ... ... I've not quite ... ...

FS (Round) 72   aah! ... ... right 42p 2
steps ...

DR   73   ... I've got at least in front of him   ... so
                  I'm now 2 steps up ... ...

D   74   let's do another 42p ... ...

FS (Comp)   75   ... if he's done 10p ... ...

DR   76   ... I've got a lead of ... ... about 80 ...

FS (Round) 77   let's try some 10ps ... ...
                  ... ... right ... ... now let's see ... 1 step ...
                  ... ...

DR   78   ... . so we've won that one ... ...

Race Number 8:

Round 1 2 3 4 5 6 7 8 910111213141516117
S's decision 0 0 2 2 2 1 2 2 1 1 1 1 1 1 1 1 1
R's decision 2 1 1 1 1 2 1 1 0 0 0 0 0 0 0 0 0
Net winnings: 112

Race 9

Race 9:   Cost of 1 Step: 2
               Cost of 2 Step: 46
               Winning Post: 5
               Prize Money: 186

RRD   79   .... right, now there is a very big difference
                  between 1 step and 2 steps ...

DR   80   .. .. we beat him last time though ... ...
                  ... ... we have some winnings ... .

RV   81   .. .. this one isn't worth winning

FS (Race)   82   ... ...having said that let's 2
                    steps ... ...

DR   83   he's done 2 ... ...

FS (Round) 84   well I'm going to have to go another 2 steps

FS (Race)   85   ... ... let's keep going ... ...

Race Number 9:

Round 1 2 3 4 5
S's decision 2 2 2 2 2
R's decision 2 2 2 2 2
Net winnings: -31

Total net winnings: 178

7. Artificial Intelligence and the Economics of Technological Change

Paul Stoneman

Introduction

This paper has two main objectives. The first is to respond to the paper by Hey and Reynolds included in this volume and the second is to investigate the relation between artificial intelligence and the economics of technological change in more general terms.

Artificial intelligence is not a subject on which I consider myself to be an expert (I consider my field of expertise to be technological change). In writing this paper I have therefore been to some extent unguided, with very little knowledge of (i) the literature (ii) the issues of importance and (iii) the best way to approach these issues. Some would claim however that there is a benefit of a priori ignorance, namely a fresh viewpoint. I would not go so far.

Most of this paper is in fact directed towards the second objective above, i.e. a general consideration of the relation between AI and the economics of technological change, with a particular emphasis on the extent to which AI is useful in addressing issues relating to technological change. The paper proceeds by first considering the extent to which AI can be used as an aid to decision-making in the technological change area. The second part of the paper is concerned with a topic that is of more interest to economists; the behaviour of systems in which economic actors are represented as artificial intelligences is explored and the contribution of such systems to economic understanding is discussed. There is a third route that could be taken in looking at the relation between AI and the economics of technological change that in essence involves the use of AI techniques to generate parameter estimates and forecasts (see, for example, Ormerod, Taylor and Walker (1990) (on neural networks). That route is not explored in this paper. The third part of the paper is a comment on the work of Hey and Reynolds. The paper closes with some conclusions.

Expert Systems

In order to proceed, a definition of AI is required. Rauch-Hindin (1987) defines AI as a 'software technique that programs use to represent data symbolically, reason with the data symbolically, and, by so doing solve symbolic, rather than numeric problems'. This is not particularly helpful. Harmon and King (1985) give a more useful definition. They are particularly concerned with expert systems (also known as knowledge systems), defined following Fiegenbaum as an 'intelligent computer program that uses knowledge and inference procedures to solve problems that are difficult enough to require significant human expertise for their solution. Knowledge necessary to perform at such a level, plus the inference procedures used, can be thought of as a model of the expertise of the best practitioners in the field.'

Although it is clear from the literature that expert systems and artificial intelligence are not synonymous, for the purposes of this paper the distinction between them is not overly important. The paper proceeds therefore, following the above definition, with a conceptualization of AI as a set of implicit and explicit rules that, taking account of information deficiencies, complexity and uncertainties etc. provides a black box from which answers to relevant questions result that mirror the decisions that would be made by an expert. With such a conceptualization throughout this paper the terms of expert system and AI are used interchangeably. It is particularly informative, however, to note the comment of Harmon and King that knowledge-based systems are aids to decision-making and not replacements for human decision-making. They are thus not, in general, automata.

It is clear from the literature on knowledge systems or expert systems that the primary effectiveness of such systems is in fields where decision-making is complex and where optimisation in explicit analytical models, the preferred tool of the neoclassical economist, is not generally available. In the absence of a clear analytical solution to problems the expert or knowledge system attempts to instead mirror the actual decision-making processes of the expert. The artificial intelligence thus created enables the non-expert to derive solutions (the solutions that the expert would have derived) for the complex problems. Coombs Saviotti and Walshe (1987) neatly encapsulate the complex nature of technologically related problems that lead one to consider that expert systems will be appropriate to the analysis of such problems:

> The discussion of the organization and execution of R&D .... has revealed a variety of management practices which appear to depend on tacit knowledge, ad hoc procedures, and accumulated experience in particular fields. These practices are set in a context of technical and market uncertainty and organizational complexity, and depend upon the actions of scientists and technologists who are still subject to an attenuated form of the collegial control mechanisms of the scientific establishment. Not surprisingly, the formal algebraic apparatus of economic analysis is not very effective in this domain (pages 88-9).

That technological change is an area typified by uncertainty, information deficiencies and complexity can be simply exemplified by discussing these in turn. First, there are three basic types of uncertainty, all of which exist in technological decision-making: (i) technical uncertainty i.e. what works or does not work, what the alternatives are etc., (ii) market uncertainty i.e. size of the potential market for any new product, general economic prospects, reception of a new product etc., and (iii) uncertainty as to rivals' reactions, for example whether rivals are researching, in what directions, and how efficient they are etc. Secondly, although the distinction between uncertainty and information deficiencies is not totally clear, there can be information deficiencies in the sense of information impactedness in that the information exists within the decision-making unit, but not in the hands of the decision-maker. For example the technologist may not have commercial information and the accountant may not have (or be able to interpret) technological information. There can also be information deficiencies in the sense of imperfect information relating to, for example, what rivals are doing, market knowledge, scientific knowledge and the effectiveness of the patent system. Finally, technological decisions can be complex for many reasons. A few examples might be inter-project dependency. the intertemporal nature of decisions, the interaction between basic and applied research and development, and in many cases the networking nature of technologies and the resulting problem of standards and infrastructure requirements.

One can argue, given this, that it is clear that the domain of technological change is one where analytical optimization is unlikely to be available for most (or many) decisions. This would seem to imply that the area of the analysis of technological change would be a fertile field in which to build expert systems and to make use of AI techniques as an aid to decision-making.

By the nature of expert systems, the questions addressed by such systems would probably need to be reasonably small and self-contained, but one could think of expert systems that would codify decision-making on a particular issue. Exactly what these issues might be is not immediately obvious, however, one might think of an expert system that would codify the decision of experts on whether to invest in Project A or Project B, or a system that might be used to generate a preferred portfolio of projects in a firm's R&D strategy, or even, given the paper by Hey and Reynolds, a system to aid decision-making relating to the speed at which a particular project is to proceed.

There is a query however, as to the extent to which such decisions are the domain of economics. They are more the domain of operational research (OR), which attempts to increase the internal efficiency of the firm. Where the domain of the OR specialist and the economist tend to overlap would be with respect to the larger questions, such as determining how much the firm should spend on R&D, and such large questions tend not to be particularly suitable to the application of expert systems. In my view, the use of AI in economics is primarily in another direction which is discussed below, but which mainly relates to the market interaction between firms (this not being the domain of the OR researcher). However, before moving to this, it is worth noting a particular problem relating to the use of expert systems for assisting such internal decisions. It is well known in the economics of technological change that the decisions made by the technologist often differ from decisions made on a commercial basis. In fact a particular issue in the area concerns ways in which to get commercial considerations to influence technological decisions. The efficiency of the use of expert systems for making such decisions is thus crucially dependent on the extent to which the objectives of the expert characterized by the expert system reflect the objectives of the firm. In many cases it is clear that they will not. (It would be an interesting exercise to see the extent of agreement between expert systems reflecting the decisions of different economists, perhaps one would achieve three systems from two economists!)

In many ways, however interesting the construction of specific expert decision systems might be, this is probably not the crux of the relationship between AI and economics. As interesting as it might be to devise a system that would generate optimal stopping rules for investments in R&D projects, for example, this appears to be only peripheral to relationship between AI and economics.

Economic Actors as Artificial Intelligences

A topic more central to the relation between AI and economics, and also of more interest, comes from another starting point. The essence of real world decision-making, especially as regards R&D, is the uncertain and complex environment in which those decisions are made (as illustrated above). In modelling the behaviour of the firm, main line economics tends to glide over these characteristics by assuming simple behavioural rules, e.g. maximization of expected profits assuming objective probabilities on outcomes. Such assumptions are not meant to be particularly accurate statements of what economic actors actually do, but rather working hypotheses that enable the derivation of precise mathematical results on issues of a higher level of interest, e.g. the impact of oligopolistic rivalry on R&D spending or the impact of an innovation on the demand curve.

How firms actually reach decisions has not in the past been of great interest to economists (although it is forecast that the future may yield much greater interest in this area, as seen in the contributions to the centenary issue of the Economic Journal, January 1991, Vol 101, No 404). Economists have been more concerned with the decisions actually reached. This is no more apparent than in the debate over the 'as if' doctrine, which might be paraphrased as it does not matter what firms actually do, as long as the assumptions of the models mirror the actual decisions made, e.g., it does not matter if firms maximize or not as long as the decisions they make are those that would be made if they did maximize.

The basic problem in trying to build models that reflect the actual decision-making behaviour of firms is that the decision making process is complex and imprecise. The economic modeller is trying to abstract from reality in order to emphasize particular issues that are relevant to the question in hand. One may recall the maxim of Joan Robinson that a model that reflects all of reality is as much use as a map of scale one to one. The art of the economic modeller is to abstract from reality, in order to concentrate on the 'fundamental issues' that are most important in the determination of the answer to the question in hand. Thus, for example, if one wishes to discuss the impact on a decision of changing attitudes to risk and uncertainty, one must incorporate uncertainty in the model. If, on the other hand, the answer to a question is the same in certain and uncertain environments, one need not incorporate the complication of uncertainty into one's model.

However, abstraction is fine if one can be sure of the accuracy of the 'as if' assumption. One way to test the assumption is to see if the empirical regularities match the predictions of the economic model based on the 'as' if assumption. There are two ways in which one can go about this. The first is to see if a number of empirical regularities are in fact generated by the model. Such empirical regularities in the area of technological change (often called stylized facts) might include (mainly taken from the list of Dasgupta (1986)): a positive association between R&D input and innovative output; that the cost of developing something seems to increase more than proportionately as development time decreases; that success breeds success; that larger firms (after some threshold level) do not engage in greater R&D relative to firm size than do smaller firms; that up to some level, industry R&D intensity increases with concentration; that there is little intertemporal variation in firms' R&D spend relative to sales; and there seems to be short termism apparent in the behaviour of firms with tendencies to cut back on R&D in recessions.

One would hope that any valid economic model would be able to generate these and other such empirical regularities as predictions. A second and more precise approach to looking at empirical validity is to use econometrics. The particular problem with validating economic models by their predictive performance is that although the empirical regularities and the predictions of the model may match, the empirical regularities will only apply to states of the world actually observed. One can never be sure that in other states of the world that the regularities will still hold i.e. the model based on the 'as if' assumption may break down in a world with different experiences than those actually observed.

If one is unwilling to rely upon econometric validation, and if the generation of stylized facts is not considered adequate validation, one can argue that the 'as if' approach itself is not valid, and as a result some detailed knowledge of the decision-making process itself will be essential to any full understanding of how firms, industries and economies behave. An early example of how such an approach has influenced economics is the work of Cyert and March (1963) on how firms actually make decisions compared to how economists assumed that decisions were made. It was often argued however that the insights deriving from such work were useful, but unfortunately the system was not operational and therefore added little to the economists' analytical armoury. Later Nelson and Winter (1982) showed that such systems could be made operational, and illustrated that a system based on evolutionary techniques could replicate the performance of the US economy as well as the simple neoclassical model of Solow (1957).

However, the Nelson and Winter paper is really no more than the modelling of an economy in which actors are modelled as expert systems. The behaviour of actors is represented by a set of rules that characterize decision-making processes, i.e. a computer-based package that provides the decision that would be made by an expert as an outcome. The model is not of a maximizing character, and it has an environment of complexity and uncertainty.

How is the work of Nelson and Winter to be viewed? One could say that the Nelson and Winter model shows that the 'as if' assumptions of neoclassical theory are OK after all, for the two systems generate the same behaviour. In which case the more complex system of Nelson and Winter is of value because it shows that economists were not on the wrong lines; but the simple system works just as well so one need not worry too much about not using the complex system and can abstract and use an 'as if' model. Alternatively, one could argue that the reason for not having a more accurate description of decision-making behaviour in economic models is that such models are too complex. The Nelson and Winter work shows, however, that if one represents actual decision-making behaviour by an expert system, then that objection is no longer a valid reason for not using such models.

Of late there has been further work in the Nelson and Winter tradition, with economic actors represented by expert systems, which explores the extent to which standard results are or are not replicated by such models. Thus instead of assuming simple behaviour on the part of firms or households, complex behaviour is assumed, but that behaviour is represented by an expert system, the functioning of which, although complex, can be computer simulated. For example, Arifovic (1989), models the learning about their environment and objective functions by economic agents using a genetic algorithm, with the result that:

> for a model in which competitive firms have to make their production decisions before observing the price of a single good in a market, the values of prices and quantities to which the algorithm converged correspond to rational expectations equilibria.

If there were any construct in economics that were of an 'as if' nature it would be rational expectations. However, this illustrates that even with uncertainty and poor information the system can generate such an equilibrium with an observation-based description of actual economic behaviour.

Use of genetic algorithms is also made by Miller (1987), who considers games played by automata, in which the strategy embodied in the automata evolves over time. In this case there appears to be little correspondence to the standard game theory results.

Brian Arthur (1990) summarizes the results of the Santa Fe research programme from which these two papers come as follows:

> [The] approach introduces into economics the possibility of 'artificial intelligence agents' that can gather information, improve their actions as they receive feedback from their environment, make sudden discoveries, and 'learn to learn' at a meta level, much as humans do.
>
> We can go further and calibrate the learning algorithm...against actual human learning data collected in the economy itself or in a corresponding laboratory learning experiment. This allows us the possibility of replacing the idealized perfectly rational agents within standard neoclassical models with 'calibrated agents' that behave in a more human-like way. We can then ask how the outcome of the problem in question might change if the 'rationality', assumed in the model replicated human rationality.
>
> When we carry out this type of exercise, we find that for certain problems that have relatively simple structures, the standard solution goes through. For other problems with more complicated structures, we find that no equilibrium, no attractors may exist. In fact, if the number of possibilities for actions and expectations in the system becomes large enough, there may be no natural end to the 'discovery' or 'emergence' of new structures or patterns.

This approach is thus replacing the standard assumption of neoclassical economics of rational actors with expert systems, and exploring how firms, industries and economies behave as those expert systems make decisions. This may seem a rather science fiction characterization of an economy, but one may think of computerized trading on stock exchanges, which is little different.

Characterizing Technological Decisions: Hey and Reynolds

If one is to think of technological decisions being made by an artificial intelligence, how would one begin to characterize those intelligences? Another way of putting this is to ask how an expert system making technological decisions would look or behave. This paper does not provide an answer to this. Although there are some hints in this paper as to how it might look, for example it should produce the empirical regularities detailed above, it is beyond the brief of this paper (and probably beyond my expertise at this time) to proceed far on this route. Instead, it is more informative at this stage to comment on the paper by Hey and Reynolds and their system.

The work of Hey and Reynolds is designed to explore the extent to which the predictions of simple game theoretic models are replicated by subjects acting under experimental conditions. This procedure is recommended by Roth (1990) as a valid method to validate some of the predictions of such theory. The paper by Roth is also a useful source of detail on other attempts to use the procedure. Hey and Reynolds then move to analysing how subjects reached their decisions, which is a further stage forward.

The Hey and Reynolds experiments relate to a simple patent-race model. The character of such races is that the first player past the winning post takes the prize. The nature of technological, and thus R&D decisions, has been characterized above as involving uncertainty, complexity and limited information. The Hey and Reynolds model, on the other hand, contains little of any of these. There is full knowledge on the part of each player, except as far as each player is ignorant as to the reactions or strategy of rivals in the game. The Hey and Reynolds experiment is mainly concerned with how each player will react to rivals' reactions and learn about the nature of such oligopolistic interaction. A particular issue is whether players will follow the optimal strategies as defined in theory.

The paper suggests that in general players do not follow the strategy that theory would predict. However, the results in the paper may be interpreted more generously (for the theory that is) as that actors take time to learn about what decisions are optimal but, as they learn, they do approach the theoretically predicted decision.

At this point it is difficult to resist quoting from Dasgupta (1986):

> Many years ago a distinguished physicist advised the world never to trust an empirical result until it is confirmed by theory.

A not unfair reading of the Hey and Reynolds results is that they are not precisely those that theory would predict. Given the above quote, who then should one trust? There does not seem to be a definitive answer.

Instead one can usefully pursue a slightly different tack. The Hey and Reynolds paper is based on a patent race. In particular, a race where all the technological information is certain. It is known how many steps are necessary to reach the winning post and the prize is also known. Are such races a reasonable way to model technological decision-making?

It is quite clear that there is an element of racing in technological decision-making, for it is also clear that with a patent system there is a sense in which it is important to be first past the winning post. However, doubts can be expressed as to whether this is a dominant issue in such decisions. The reasons for this are clear

a)   It is generally accepted that except in the pharmaceutical industry (where other issues arise that weaken the support for a race framework), the patent system rarely acts as an efficient protector of technological knowledge (see Mansfield (1981)).

b)   Even if the patent system were effective, patents are issued when technologies are far from the market and the development expenditures are still to be incurred. Much of the R&D spend will thus not be protected by patents.

c)   It is not at all clear that the first technologies to market win the prize. There may be standards problems (as with video recorders where VHS was not first to market but eventually dominated), or there may be advantages in being a fast second. The moral to be learned from the EMI experience of body scanners is often quoted here, as might be the experience of the Comet.

d)   It is also clear that technology per se does not win a market, there is still the issue of production efficiency and marketing etc.

Such comments considerably limit the faith one can place in the modelling of R&D as a race. There is however a more basic problem in the use of such frameworks that is detailed and discussed by Dasgupta (1986). The nature of the race is that the firm faces a discontinuity in its returns to R&D. Such discontinuities will really only exist in the absence of uncertainty. The argument is best put in Dasgupta's own words:

> Such discontinuous games ...are really rather spurious. They hint at something but they are also misleading. Tournaments distinguish winners and losers sharply, but on their own they do not make for discontinuous games. One requires in addition the hypothesis that firms face uncertainties that are perfectly correlated. If they are not, then, in general, no firm can be certain of being the winner - no matter how much effort it puts in - unless it can make it unprofitable for rivals to enter the race. Firms in such circumstances will choose probability distributions whose parameters are affected by R&D effort. Typically, their expected profits will be continuous functions. The resulting games reflecting technological competition are therefore continuous (p.160).

This, and the comments above, lead one to the conclusion that discontinuous races are not an ideal way to begin the modelling of technological competition.

Even if this is not accepted, one still needs to explore the contribution that the Hey and Reynolds paper makes to our understanding of the relation between AI and the economics of technological change. In the paragraphs above it has been argued that a major issue of concern is whether the representation of the complex decision-making processes of individuals by models of artificial intelligences can contribute to the understanding of the process of technological change. It is not obvious that the Hey and Reynolds paper adds very much at all to this debate.

Conclusions

As stated above, the initial purpose of this paper was to comment on the work of Hey and Reynolds. The brief of the paper was however extended to encompass a consideration in more general terms of the relation between AI and the economics of technological change.

There are valid arguments for supporting the view that there is a role for the construction of expert systems as aids to firm decision-making in the area of technological change (for well-specified limited questions), but such models are more the domain of OR than Economics. There may also be a role for the use of AI techniques, such as neural networks, for statistical and forecasting purposes.

Of most interest, however, is the behaviour of economic systems where actors are represented by expert systems or artificial intelligences. Such representations allow a more accurate reflection of the complexity of individual behaviour than is common in economic modelling. Here the main issue is whether such systems can predict empirical regularities, and if they can do so, whether they yield any extra insights over and above those of 'as if' models. It is clear that if the predictions as to economic behaviour are the same as in 'as if' models then, for many purposes, the complex systems are unnecessary. In the discussion above it is argued that sometimes different answers result, in other cases they do not. However, even if the answers are not different, this does not mean that the pursuit of complex systems is irrelevant. Such research can illuminate the process by which decisions are made, but in addition if it is confirmed that the simple models yield correct predictions, that information will be of great value to the mass of economists who would prefer to stick to their simple analytical models rather than to construct large scale models requiring computer simulation in order to answer each and every question.

It was argued above that the extent to which an economic model needs to be complex and reflect all aspects of reality depends upon the questions to be answered with that model. There is a danger that if one goes too far down the route of arguing that all decisions are complex and thus need to be modelled as such, one will reject all results derived from simple models. This would be a retrograde step. Over the years we have learnt a great deal about the nature of the economics of technological change on the basis of simple models that would appear to be robust. Thus, for example, the advances of knowledge relating to the nature of information, market failures, strategic competition and the welfare aspects of policy, among others, are useful and valid contributions to knowledge. To argue that these have to be rejected because they are derived from too simple a decision theoretic base would be a mistake.

If nothing else comes from the above discussion, it appears to be valid to argue that what economists need to know, both in the area of technological change and all other areas of economics, basically relates to the appropriate level of abstraction for modelling. As was argued above, if complex models provide the same answers as simple models, then for many purposes the simple models will do. If not, then a more complex approach is required. Even if there is no other contribution to economics from the use of AI, some insight into the appropriate level of model complexity would be a more than sufficiently valuable contribution to merit further work in the area.

8. Some Thoughts on Economic Theory and Artificial Intelligence

Huw Dixon

Introduction

In this paper I will offer some thoughts on the potential contribution of artificial intelligence to economic theory. I write as someone who is at present an orthodox economic theorist and who has only recently been introduced to the ideas and achievements of modern artificial intelligence. My overall impression is that artificial intelligence does have a potential to offer economic theory, both in terms of providing a fruitful perspective from which to view currently problematic issues, and through raising new and interesting problems that have been hitherto marginalized or ignored.

In my view, the main potential contribution of artificial intelligence to economic theory lies in providing a practical methodology for modelling reasoning, and hence rationality. Economic decision-making is one of many human activities which can be said to display 'intelligence', since it involves potentially complex reasoning and problem-solving. Artificial intelligence is a branch of computing which aims to design machines which can perform such 'intelligent' activities; as such, it has much to say about how humans go about solving problems. There now exists a wide body of research on artificial intelligence in a variety of applications which may well prove useful to economic theorists.

However, the current orthodox approach of economic theory to rationality is well-established and simple. Advocates of artificial intelligence need to demonstrate clearly why there is a need to change perspective, and how it will pay off in terms of theoretical understanding. Therefore in Section 1 I explore both the current orthodox model of 'rationality without reasoning', and in particular I consider to what extent it can be extended to embrace 'bounded rationality'. As I will argue, I believe that by generalizing strict optimization to approximate optimization we can maintain the simplicity of the current orthodoxy without needing explicitly to model problem-solving with artificial-intelligence techniques.   In section 2 I take the more positive approach of considering how artificial-intelligence techniques can make a useful contribution in modelling the behaviour of economic agents in complex decision situations.   In particular, I describe the use of finite automata to model the complexity of strategies, and also the issues arising from the choice of strategies.   To put matters very simply, insofar as agents tend to 'get things right' in the sense of choosing an action or solution close to the optimum, we (as economists) need not really worry about how the decision is arrived at.   The role for artificial intelligence seems to me to have the greatest potential in situations where agents make mistakes.   This potential is, of course, of great relevance to the study of disequilibrium, an area of economics that has proven notoriously difficult within the orthodox model of rationality.   Lastly, in Section 3, I consider the implications of modelling reasoning in strategic environments.   Insofar as the method of solving a problem might influence the action you choose, reasoning itself can be a method of precommitment.   This is illustrated in the context of Cournot duopoly.

I would like to acknowledge my debt to the writings of Herbert Simon: whilst I have not referenced his works explicitly in detail, his ideas were formative in my education and have clearly influenced the way I look at things.

Orthodox Economic Rationality: Rationality without Reasoning

At the heart of orthodox economics beats a model of rationality. The economic conception of rationality has become embodied by the mathematical theory of constrained optimization. Put at its simplest, a rational agent is conceived of as choosing the best option open to him, given his constraints.   The historical basis of this lies in utilitarianism, and in particular the Utilitarian psychology of individual action, which saw mankind placed 'under the governance of two sovereign masters, pain and pleasure' (Bentham, (1789, p.33)).   Although more recently economics has eschewed utilitarian psychology due to problems of measurement of cardinal utilities, the notion of maximization itself has become, if anything, more central. If we consider the salient features of economic rationality, three points are worth highlighting in the present context.

(1) There is no modelling of reasoning. The process or procedure of reasoning is viewed as unimportant in itself, and the outcome inevitable. If a solution (maximum) exists, then the rational agent will arrive at that solution; agents costlessly choose their best option. (2) Technical assumptions are made to ensure that a well-defined maximum exists. This usually involves two sorts of assumptions. First, to ensure that a well-defined continuous objective function can be specified; second, to ensure that the agents choice set is compact. It is often easy to forget how many assumptions are made by economists just to ensure both of these criteria are satisfied, so as to ensure the existence of a maximum. (3) If it is not possible to impose plausible restrictions to ensure the existence of a well-defined maximum, there exists no obvious, typical, or generally accepted solution to the problem.

Let us illustrate this with reference to standard consumer theory. A household is assumed to have preferences over possible outcomes, which are taken to be suitably defined bundles of commodities which it might consume. These preferences are 'represented' by a utility function, which assigns to each bundle a real number, with the property that bundles which are preferred have higher numbers. If we turn to the first issue, a well-defined utility function is ensured by four assumptions: (i) the 'sanity clause' of reflexivity that each bundle is at least as good as itself; (ii) that preferences are complete, so that any two bundles can be compared to each other; (iii) that preferences are transitive, so that if A is preferred to B, and B to C, then A is preferred to C; (iv) continuity, so that if one bundle is strictly preferred to another, there is a bundle in between that is also strictly preferred. It should be noted that the assumptions of transitivity and continuity in particular are required only for mathematical reasons, rather than any fundamental notions of rationality. The second issue of compactness is rather easier to ensure: the household is restricted to choosing its utility-maximizing bundle from its budget set, which is closed and bounded (at least if all prices are strictly positive).

The main feature of the orthodox model of economic rationality is that there is no modelling of the reasoning processes of agents, or of how decisions are reached. The formal maximization process is simply stated, and if a maximum exists it is assumed that an action yielding the maximum is chosen. This can be seen as a model of rationality without reasoning, a 'black box' or even 'empty box' approach to behaviour. The great attraction of the approach is that it means that economic theory can largely ignore the potentially complex and diverse processes of reasoning and decision-making underlying the behaviour of individual economic agents and organizations. This yields a very simple model of rationality. Whilst it has been criticized for its very simplicity, in that it ignores much real-world complexity, it has certainly delivered results and proven itself in many contexts.

In order to convince economists of its value, advocates of artificial intelligence need to demonstrate that there is both a clear need and payoff to model reasoning itself.

Whilst simplicity is perhaps the most cogent defence of orthodox economic rationality, another important defence is that it can easily be extended to encompass bounded rationality. Given that some economic environments are complex and uncertain, so that strictly defined optimizing may be inappropriate, it still may be unnecessary to deviate from the orthodox model. Whatever line of reasoning, search procedure, or algorithm agents may use, rational agents may be reasonably assumed to get 'near' to the strictly defined optimum. A very simple way to model this is to assume that agents ϵ-optimize: they choose an action that yields them within ϵ of their best payoff. Let us specify this a little more formally. Suppose that an agent chooses an action, a, that is chosen from the closed interval [0,A], and that its payoff function $U_i:[0,A] \to R$ is continuous. Then there exists a maximum, U^*, which is yielded by some a^*:

$$a^* = \text{argmax } U(a)$$

This is depicted in Fig. 1, where the optimal a^* is assumed unique. It might be argued that in a particular context the agent will not be

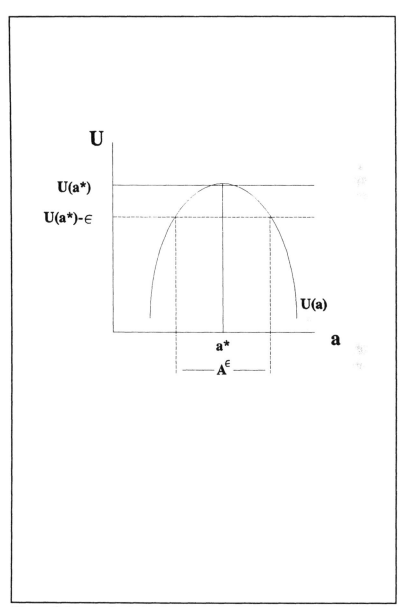

Figure 8.1   *ε-Optimization*

willing or able to inevitably choose a*. Rather, the agent might adopt some heuristic search procedure or rule of thumb that might get reasonably close to optimum in terms of payoff. The details of the precise line of reasoning taken need not (it can be argued) concern the economist. Rather, whatever the route taken, the agent can be said to be ϵ-maximizing, or choosing actions which yield payoffs within ϵ of the maximum. Given the continuity of U(.), there will in general be a set of such acceptable solutions, defined for $\epsilon > 0$ by:

$$A^\epsilon = \{a\epsilon[0,A]: U(a) \geq U^* - \epsilon\}$$

This set is depicted in Fig. 1. Two points need making. Firstly, the concept of ϵ-maximization is a generalization of strict optimization: a* is always an acceptable solution, and when $\epsilon = 0$ it is the only acceptable solution. Secondly, the choice of ϵ is more or less arbitrary, although it is usually taken to be more acceptable if it is 'small'.

A simple generalization of the orthodox approach is thus sufficient to capture some elements of bounded rationality without the need explicitly to model reasoning. As in the case of strict optimisation, approximate optimization goes straight from the statement of the problem to the set of approximate solutions. Corresponding to the notion of ϵ-maximization is the notion of an ϵ-equilibrium. For example, a Nash ϵ-equilibrium is defined in much the same way as a 'strict' Nash equilibrium. Suppose now that there are two agents, i = 1, 2, choosing actions ai from compact strategy sets A_i, and continuous payoff functions U_i (a_1, a_2). An ϵ-equilibrium occurs when both players choose actions (a_1^*, a_2^*) which yield them within ϵ of their best payoff given the action of the other player. Formally, for player 1 (and analogously for 2) (a_1^*, a_2^*) satisfies:

$$U_1 (a_1^*, a_2^*) \geq U_1 (a_1, a_2^*) - \epsilon \quad \text{for all } a_1 \in A_1$$

This can be represented by 'reaction functions', where a reaction correspondence gives the player actions that yield within ϵ of his best response given the other player's action. For player 1, we have $r_1:A_2$

$\Rightarrow A_1$:

$$r_1(a_2) = \{a_1 \epsilon A_1: U_1 (a_1, a_2) \geq \text{argmax } U_1 (a_1, a_2) -\epsilon\}$$

These reaction correspondences are 'fat' because there is a set of ϵ-maximal responses to any action by the other agent. An ϵ-equilibrium occurs at any point in the intersection of the two reaction correspondences, as depicted in Fig. 2. It should be noted en passant that in general there will be many (in the 'continuum' sense) ϵ-equilibria, and they may well be Pareto-ranked. To see this, merely consider what happens as ϵ gets large: for ϵ large enough, any conceivable outcome will be an ϵ-equilibrium! However, whilst multiplicity is endemic to ϵ-equilibria, it is not exclusive. There is no real reason why there should be unique strict optima and unique equilibria in strict Nash equilibria. They are usually ruled out for convenience sake, because models with unique and well-behaved equilibria are simpler to deal with.

The concept of bounded rationality as embodied in the notions of approximate optimization and equilibria, whilst not in general usage, is certainly not uncommon. Well known recent examples include Akerlof and Yellen's work on business cycles (Akerlof and Yellen (1985)), and Radner's work on cooperation in the finitely repeated prisoner's dilemma (Radner (1980)). The notion of ϵ-equilibrium has been often used when no strict equilibrium exists (see, inter alia, Hart (1979), Dixon (1987)).

The notion of ϵ-optimization is a simple generalization of strict-optimization that maintains its parsimony. The details of reasoning need not be considered, and it is not mathematically difficult to deal with. However, there still seems to me to be further conceptually simple extensions of the more-or-less orthodox that can be used to try and capture aspects of bounded rationality without the need to model reasoning. One possibility that has not (I believe) been explored, is to treat the rational player's decision as a type of mixed strategy. The decision-making process might have general properties: it would be more likely to choose a better outcome; it might be able to avoid payoffs that are sufficiently bad, and so on. Again, this would be a generalization of strict-optimization (which puts a probability of one on the maximal, and zero elsewhere).

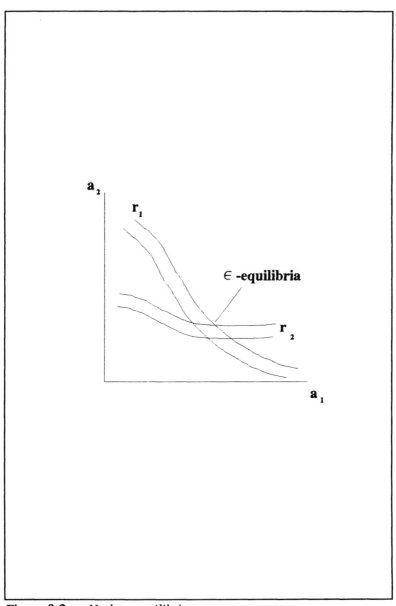

Figure 8.2   *Nash ∈-equilibria*

138

Whilst this approach has not been pursued, I believe it to be indicative of the fact that there are many possible extensions to the orthodox model that maintain its key advantages of simplicity and parsimony. The task for artificial intelligence is to show that it can yield something more than can be obtained by developing the orthodox approach.

Complexity and artificial intelligence

I have described orthodox economic rationality as 'rationality without reasoning'. If a problem is sufficiently simple and well defined so that there exists a solution which is easily computable, the precise method of solution adopted may not matter. For example, a non-singular square matrix can be inverted by different techniques, all of which will yield the same solution. However, for complicated problems it may be the case that although we know a solution (optimum) exists, we do not know how to find it with certainty. Even worse, we may not know if a solution exists at all. In such a situation, the precise form of reasoning may be important, because it will determine the types of actions or decisions arrived at. In this context I am equating 'reasoning' with a particular method of searching for a solution (an algorithm). More importantly, different methods of searching for a solution may tend to yield different types of outcomes. In this context the choice of reasoning itself can become a strategic decision, as I will discuss in the next section.

There are two dimensions of complexity that deserve the particular consideration of economists, which I will outline in this section. Firstly, there is the complexity of strategies; secondly, there is the complexity of choice of strategies. I shall now briefly discuss these two issues.

Taking a cue from standard game theory, a strategy can be seen as a rule for choosing actions, in which the action chosen is a function of the information available to an agent. At any time, the 'information' available might be taken to consist of all of the past actions of various players, plus the realizations of various exogenous parameters. For example, an oligopolist at time t, might know the history of play up to time t, in the sense of knowing all the choices of outputs by itself and other firms, as well as (for example) the past realizations of demand. If we denote this 'history' at time t as h_t, a strategy is a rule (or in mathematical terms, a mapping) that tells the firm at any time t what action to take given h_t:

$$x_t = r (h_t, t)$$

In informal terms, the strategy can be seen as a 'game plan' for the firm, telling it what to do in every possible contingency. In standard game theory, there is no limit to the complexity of the strategies chosen by agents. Furthermore, some of the results of game theory require very complicated strategies to support equilibria (for example, the 'carrot and stick' punishment strategies supporting equilibria in Folk theorems).

Various authors (Rubenstein (1986), Abreu and Rubenstein (1988), Kalai and Stanford (1988)) have argued that some limits or constraints need to be put on the complexity of strategies chosen. A popular way of capturing 'complexity' in this context is to use the notion of a 'Moore machine' or 'finite automaton' as a way of representing a strategy. A finite automaton is a machine with a finite set of states, and a specified initial state. It then has two rules: one specifies what action it takes at time t as a function of its state at time t; the second is a transition rule which specifies what its state in time t + 1 will be as a function of both its state in time t and the action of the other player at time t. The size of the automaton (its 'computing power') is captured by the number of states it has: '... the complexity of a strategy will be identical with the size (number of states) of the smallest automaton which is able to implement it'. (Kalai and Stanford (1988)).

This can easily be illustrated by a couple of examples using 'transition diagrams' to represent the automaton (see Rubenstein (1986) for a full and lucid exposition). Let us take the standard prisoner's dilemma game, where there are two agents, i = 1, 2, each with two strategies, C (cooperate) and D (defect), with payoffs as in Table 1. The automaton can be represented by $< Q_i, q^0, \lambda_i, \mu_i >$ where Q_i is the set of states; $q^0 \epsilon Q_i$ is the initial state; λ_i gives the action a_i as a function of state q_i, and μ_i is the transition rule giving next period's state. The simplest strategy is generated by a 'one-state' machine, where $Q_i = q^0 = Q$, $\mu(Q) = Q$, and either $\lambda_i (Q) = C$ or $\lambda_i (Q) = D$. That is, a 'one-state' machine can only cooperate (or defect) all of the time: because it only has one state it can only ever choose one action, as depicted in Fig. 3a. In order to respond, the automaton requires more states and more complicated transition rules. Let us consider a two-state machine, with one state, q^D, for defection, and one, q^c, for cooperation. The 'tit-for-tat' strategy is when the player cooperates until the other player defects, in which case he punishes the defection by playing D himself for one period before returning to C (see Axelrod (1984)). The automaton implementing this strategy is represented in Fig. 3b, and is defined by a set of states $Q = \{q^c, q^D\}$, initial state $q^0 = q^c$, action rule $\lambda (q^i) = a$ $(a = D, S)$, and transition rule $\mu(q, a) = q_i$ $(a = D, S)$. The 'grim' punishment strategy punishes a defection forever, and is represented in Fig. 3c. The 'grim punishment' automaton has an initial state, q^c. If the other automaton ever plays D, the machine switches to its defect state q^D, where it remains forever. The main point is that the automaton with more states can implement more complicated strategies.

		Player 2	
		C	D
Player 1	C	2, 2	0, 3
	D	3, 0	1, 1

Table 8.1 *Prisoner's dilemma*

Using the model of a finite automaton to represent a strategy, Rubenstein et al have represented a game as involving agents choosing machines rather than strategies. The players 'optimize'

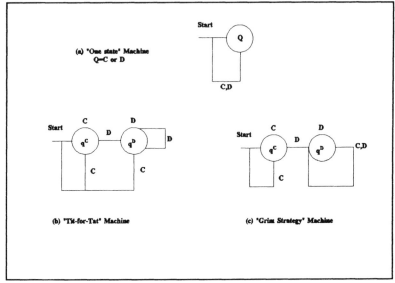

Figure 8.3   Strategies as finite automata

over the choice of their machines (strategies), and then the machines play the game.   As such, this approach ignores issues of computational complexity, and focuses merely on the issue of implementational complexity. Abreu and Rubenstein (1988) draw the analogy of sophisticated managers formulating simple operating rules for the firm.

The issue of computational complexity is central to artificial intelligence.   Some problems are simple enough to have a deterministic method which will (nearly) always arrive at a solution. Consider the 'travelling salesman' problem:

> A salesman has a list of cities, each of which he must visit exactly once.   There are direct roads between each pair of cities on the list.   Find the route the salesman should follow so that he travels the shortest possible distance on a round trip, starting at any one of the cities and then returning there.

The solution to this problem can be found simply by exploring the 'tree' of all the possible paths, and picking the shortest one. This 'brute force' method will work, but it becomes very expensive in terms of computational requirements. With N cities, there are (N-1)! different routes: each route has N stretches. The total time required to explore the entire tree is then of order N! - with only 10 cities this method clearly becomes very lengthy (10! is 3,625,800). This is known as the phenomenon of combinatorial explosion. Since computations are not costless, rational agents need to trade-off the computational cost of a decision or search procedure with the benefits in terms of the eventual payoff. The notion of efficiency is important here: a search process is more efficient if it obtains a higher payoff (on average) for the same or fewer computations (on average). Evolving efficient search strategy involves using heuristics, which are guides or short-cuts that we believe will get us near enough to the solution with reasonable computational requirements. For example, the travelling salesman problem can be solved using the useful general purpose heuristic of the nearest neighbour algorithm:

1.   Select any city as your starting point.
2.   To select the next city, consider the cities not yet visited. Go to the city closest to the one you are currently at.
3.   Repeat 2 until all of the cities have been visited.

This algorithm requires far fewer computations than 'brute force': we need to visit N cities, and at each stage we need to consider the distances between where we are and the as yet unvisited cities, of which there will be on average (N-1)/2. Computational time is therefore proportional to N(N-1)/2, or more simply N^2, which is far superior to N!. The nearest neighbour algorithm need not yield the shortest route. Bentley and Saxe (1980) have found empirical evidence that when cities are distributed at random it performs on average about 20% below the optimum. Much of practical artificial intelligence involves the construction and evaluation heuristic search procedures (see, for example, Polya's classic (1957)).

One response to the issue of computational cost and decision-making is to maintain the notion of maximizing behaviour, but simply to add in a constraint reflecting costs of decision, computation or whatever. This may be reasonable in particular applications. For example, much of standard theory assumes that it is costless to change or adjust variables.   It is simple enough in principle to introduce costs of decision or adjustment into our economic models (see, for example, Dixon (1987) for a discussion of menu costs). However, this approach cannot answer the general problem. If one is unable to solve a simple optimization problem A, it is unlikely that one can solve the more difficult problem, of optimizing A subject to some computational constraint. Super-optimization is not the answer to an initial failure of optimization.   Rather, agents are forced to adopt reasonable decision procedures rather than the optimal.

The notion that many fundamental economic decisions are complex and uncertain has of course a long pedigree in economics, with its notions of rules of thumb (see Cyert and March (1963), Hall and Hitch (1951), Simon (1957) inter alia). However, as I argued in the previous section, we can relax the assumption of strict-optimization to ϵ-optimization, which still largely maintains the 'empty box' methodology of rationality without reasoning. If agents use various heuristic techniques or rules of thumb, then presumably they will yield payoffs that are close to the optimal in some sense. In this case the precise nature of the heuristic need not bother us. The argument is really no different than in the case of 'perfect rationality', where we can predict the optimal choice irrespective of the method of solution. The only difference is that whereas the orthodox approach predicts that agents arrive at an optimal solution, we can relax this to a prediction that the agent will arrive close to the solution.

If economics is to abandon its model rationality without reasoning, it needs to be shown that there is a need to look at reasoning itself. In a complex decision problem, we may not be able to find a solution or optimum with certainty, and indeed may not even know if a solution exists. The method of reasoning, or searching for a solution may in these circumstances be important, because it will determine the actions and decisions of agents, and hence different methods may yield (or tend to yield) different types of outcomes. If we are not confident that the method of reasoning will tend to yield solutions close to the optimum, then the matter is different. I believe that the method of reasoning becomes most important when we need to understand and explain why agents make decisions that deviate considerably from the optimum. Almost paradoxically, reasoning is important only when it leads to mistakes. We only need to understand the mechanics of the rational agent's decision process when they fail.

Let me illustrate this with the example of Section 1, where an agent has to maximize a continuous function, U(a), over the interval [0, A]. Suppose that the function is as depicted in Fig. 4. We can see that analytically there exists a unique global optimum at a*: this is the choice predicted by standard economic theory. Approximate optimization would perhaps predict a point close to a*. However, suppose that our agent is in the situation of having to optimize without knowing what U looks like. He can compute the particular value of U at particular point a ϵ [0,A], and its gradient (or whatever) if defined, but only at a cost. The problem is rather like that of an econometrician trying to maximize a complicated non-linear likelihood function. There are different ways of going about this sort of problem, all of which are considered 'reasonable'. Several methods are variants of hill-climbing algorithms, as used from a point a_0 chosen at random (or by informed guess). You then compute both the value of the function and the gradient at that point: $U(a_0)$ and $U'(a_0)$. You then move a certain distance (perhaps specified by you) in the direction of steepest ascent. You stop when the function is sufficiently 'flat' and concave: usually this is defined by some pre-defined tolerance $d > 0$, so that 'flat' means $|U'| < d$. Depending on the costs of computing relative to likely gains, you may wish to start several ascents from different points. Two points are worth noting about such search procedures. Firstly, they will almost always fail to reach the solution A*: {a*} is a singleton in the interval [0,A], and is of measured zeros, and hence in a loose but clear way, a* will almost certainly never be chosen. However, as more and more points are computed, the sample maximum will tend towards the global maximum (this is ensured by the continuity of U(a)). For a survey of econometric applications see Quandt (1983, chapter 12).

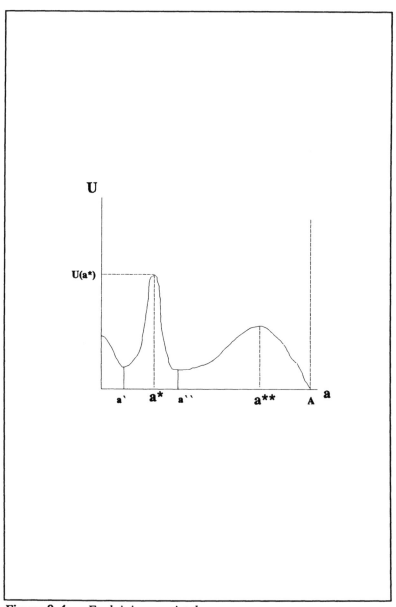

Figure 8.4   *Explaining a mistake*

The shortcomings of hill-climbing algorithms are well known (and concern 'spikes', 'ridges' and 'plateaux'). It is clearly an 'intelligent' search process that is more efficient than random search. However, depending on what the functions to be maximized look like, hill-climbing may or may not be expected to get close to the optimum. Let us consider the example of Fig. 4: there are three local optima $\{0, a^*, a^{**}\}$. If the agent starts to hill-climb in the interval $[0, a^1]$ he will tend towards 0; in the interval $[a^1, a"]$, he will tend towards the global optimum a^*; if $[a" , A]$ he will tend towards a^{**} (assuming that at points $\{a^1, a"\}$ the hill-climbing routine is eqully likely to go in either direction). Our prediction of the agents eventual choice of action would depend upon the number of computations available. However, if $[a^1, a"]$ is small relative to $[0,A]$, we would certainly need to put a positive probability on all actions close to each local optimum. Furthermore, as drawn, it is clear that if only a few computations are made, then it is much more likely that the largest value computed will be close to $U(a^{**})$, since $[a", A]$ is much larger than $[0,a^1]$ or $[a^1, a"]$.

Suppose that we observed an agent choosing action a^{**}, how might we explain it? Orthodox strict-optimization would be powerless: the optimum is $U(a^*)$, and it has not been chosen. The mistake is inexplicable. In practice, no doubt, the route of super-optimization would be pursued: the agent had a set of priors over $U(\cdot)$ and chose a^{**} to maximize the expected payoff. However, super-optimization is not an adequate response to the failure of optimization in the face of computational complexity. However, if we abandon the option of rationality without reasoning, matters are easier to explain: 'our agent adopted a hill-climbing algorithm. Given a limited number of commutations this was quite likely to end of near a^{**}. This can be explained even though a^{**} is nowhere near the optimal choice a^*, and $U(a^{**})$ is only half $U(a^*)$.

It is worth pausing here to state this argument so far, and put it in context. First, economists need not concern themselves with how economic agents solve problems if those agents successfully optimize or near optimize. We can explain and predict their behaviour as the solution of an optimization or ϵ-optimization problem. If, however, agents make 'mistakes' by choosing actions that are far from the optimal, and/or yield payoffs significantly below the maximum, matters are rather different. Then, in order to explain the specific choice, we will need to model the reasoning underlying the choice. I have given the example of a hill-climbing algorithm yielding a sub-optimal local maximum. Again, if we consider applying the nearest neighbour algorithm to the travelling salesman problem, from some starting points it will yield terrible solutions. The role for artificial intelligence in economics would then seem primarily to be in situations where economic agents make mistakes, and possibly bad mistakes. This is in some ways a paradoxical role for artificial intelligence.

However, it is a role with great potential, not least in modelling disequilibrium. I have discussed the concept of equilibrium elsewhere at some length, where the reader is referred for the details (Dixon, 1990). There are perhaps three properties that define equilibrium: firstly agents' actions are consistent (in some sense the actions of different agents 'add up'); secondly, agents are behaving optimally in equilibrium, and so have no incentive to deviate from their equilibrium actions; and thirdly, the equilibrium is the outcome of some adjustment process. If we focus on the second property, in a Nash equilibrium, each agent's actions i optimal give the action of other agents. In disequilibrium, however, agents' actions need neither be consistent, nor optimal. This causes agents to revise and adjust their behaviour, which may (or may not) drive the economic system under consideration towards equilibrium. It is the essence of disequilibrium that agents make mistakes. For this reason, the analysis of disequilibrium has been very problematic for economics. There seems to me to be a role for artificial intelligence in modelling disequilibrium systems, by specifying the decision rules used by economic agents. The firm, for example, can be viewed as an 'expert system' which will have some capacity for performing well in a variety of equilibrium and disequilibrium situations, but which may perform badly in others. Indeed, the standard 'myopic' adjustment rule used by Cournot in his analysis of stability can be thought of as just such a decision rule. The firm treats the output of the other as fixed and optimizes against it. In disequilibrium this may not be a good decision rule, although in equilibrium it may be 'reasonable'.

Reasoning as Precommitment: An Example

In the previous section I argued that artificial intelligence has a role in economics to explain how agents make mistakes in disequilibrium. In disequilibrium a perfectly reasonable decision rule may lead an agent to make sub-optimal decisions. As agents adjust their behaviour in response to such mistakes, there will (perhaps) be a movement towards equilibrium. In this section we will reverse the line of reasoning. In a strategic situation (e.g. oligopoly), there may be an incentive for firms to make 'mistakes'. In this case, agents may wish to adopt forms of reasoning that lead to actions which are in some strategic sense 'desirable', although they might in another sense not be optimal.

Perhaps the most important impact of artificial intelligence on economics will be that in modelling reasoning, it brings reasoning itself into the domain of choice, and hence opens it to strategic considerations. If an agent is perfectly rational, his behaviour is in a sense thereby restricted to a particular action (or set of actions), and hence becomes predictable. Given that a firm's objective is to maximize profits, it will choose its 'optimal' profit-maximizing price/output. Even if it were in the strategic interests of the firm to do otherwise, the rational firm is 'unable' to do anything other than the optimal. This is essentially the insight that lies behind the concepts of subgame perfection and dynamic inconsistency. In each period, agents are restricted to behaving optimally; this fact can then be used to predict their behaviour and hence the future course and outcome of play.

However, suppose that we drop the assumption of rational intuition, that if a solution exists to a problem the rational agent intuits it directly. Suppose instead that an agent has to choose how to solve a problem. The choice of how he chooses to solve a problem, his decision rule, will determine (to some extent) his eventual choice of action. Economic agents can therefore use their choice of decision algorithm as a form of precommitment to certain actions. As is well known, in a wide class of games there is an incentive for firms to precommit themselves.

This is perhaps best illustrated by an example, for which I will use Cournot duopoly. I have discussed this elsewhere, in terms of economic significances (Dixon (1988)) as well as its general significance as an equilibrium concept (Dixon (1990)). There are two firms, $i = 1, 2$, who choose outputs $X_i \geq 0$. Given these quantities, the price P clears the market via the inverse demand curve $P(X_1 + X_2)$, giving each firm i's profits as a function of both outputs (assuming costless production):

$$U_i(X_1, X_2) = X_i\, P(X_1 + X_2)$$

A Nash equilibrium is defined as a pair of outputs $(X_1{}^*, X_2{}^*)$ such that each firm is choosing its profit-maximizing output given the other firm's output. Formally:

$$X_1{}^* = \text{argmax } U_1(X_1, X_2{}^*)$$

and similarly for firm 2. In this sense then, neither firm has an incentive to deviate given the other firm's choice. This is often represented in terms of reaction functions. Firm 1's reaction function, r, gives its profit-maximizing output as a function of firm 2's reaction function (and likewise for firm 2):

$$X_1 = r_1(X_2) = \text{argmax } U_1(X_1, X_2)$$

The Nash equilibrium $(X_1{}^*, X_2{}^*)$ occurs where both firms are on their reaction-functions, i.e. $X_1{}^* = r_1(X_2{}^*)$ and $X_2{}^* = r_1(X_1{}^*)$. This is depicted in Fig. 5 at point N. Without precommitment, both firms have to be on their reaction-functions, since it is assumed that firms are rational optimizers. However, if a firm can precommit itself to take any action, then it need not be on its best-response function. As is well known, if firm 1 can precommit itself to a larger output than $X_1{}^*$, it can increase its profits by moving down the other firm's reaction-function. Under standard assumptions the maximum profit for firm 1 to earn is at its Stackelburg point, S, to the right of N. At S, firm 1 is earning higher profits than it earned at N. There is thus an incentive to precommit. However, in the absence of precommitment, X_1^* is not a credible output for firm 1 to produce, since X_1^* is not the profit-maximizing response to X_2^* (which is X_1'). In the absence of some form of precommitment, both firms are 'restricted' to being on their reaction-functions, which result in the Nash equilibrium, N.

In standard economic models, with perfectly rational agents, precommitment has tended to be thought of in terms of some irreversible act or expenditure (e.g. investment in Brander and Spencer (1983), or delegation in Vickers (1985)). However, in the case of bounded rationality, matters are rather different. Firms can choose decision-making rules that tend to yield certain outcomes. For example, in Cournot duopoly the firms have an incentive to precommit to an output larger than their profit-maximizing Nash output, since this moves them towards their Stackelburg point. Thus firms might wish to adopt decision algorithms that tend to yield large outputs, that result in systematic over-production relative to the 'optimum'. For example, if firms adopt some sort of hill-climbing algorithm, they can bias the solution to be above the optimum by tending to choose large outputs as initial positions. Such algorithms need to be told not only where to start, but when to stop. As mentioned in the previous section, the latter can be specified in terms of a threshold gradient: stop searching when the gradient falls below a certain level, $|U_i'| < d$. By starting from relatively large outputs and choosing a large d, the firm can precommit itself to choosing relatively large outputs.

Conclusion

In this paper I have sought to achieve two objectives. Firstly, to state and defend the orthodox model of economic rationality. In particular, I wanted to explore the extent to which the orthodox approach has been and can be extended to embrace the notion of bounded rationality. Secondly, given this extended notion of orthodox rationality, I sought to explore what role artificial intelligence might have in economic theory. To conclude, I will simply summarize and restate the arguments of the paper in a

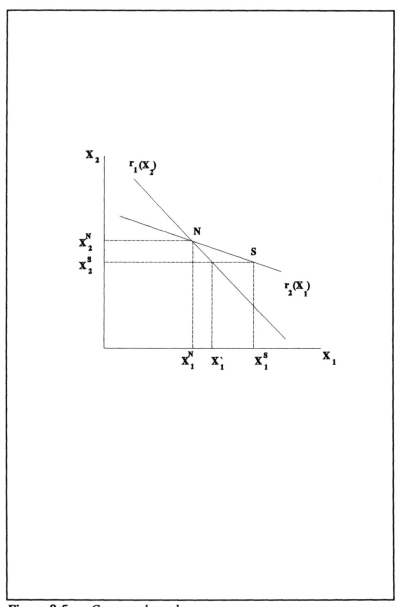

Figure 8.5   *Cournot duopoly*

schematic form.

Orthodox economic rationality is a model of rationality without reasoning. Insofar as economic agents tend to get things right - or almost right - we do not as theorists need to model how they solve their constrained-optimization problems. In most economic models it is assumed that agents are 'strict' optimizers, who effortlessly optimize. Whilst this is an idealization/simplification, it can easily be generalized to embrace bounded rationality by adopting the notion of ϵ-optimization. In neither case is it necessary to consider in detail how agents actually decide what to do, their 'reasoning'. This is an advantage insofar as it means that economic theorists can avoid the complexities of the psychological and bureaucratic decision processes within individuals and organizations, and simply consider the objective problems (and solutions) themselves.

Given this extended notion of orthodox rationality, what role is there left for artificial intelligence? If orthodox rationality can handle decisions that yield optimal or near-optimal outcomes, it would appear that the main area for artificial intelligence to make a distinctive contribution is in situations where agents do not take decisions that yield optimal or near-optimal outcomes. I have highlighted two particular areas of possible research where this may be necessary: disequilibrium and strategic environments. In disequilibrium environments it is of the essence that agents make mistakes (otherwise we would be in equilibrium). For this very reason economic theorists have had great difficulty in modelling disequilibrium. In order to explain mistakes we need to understand not only the problem faced by agents, but the reasoning of agents, their method of solution. Artificial intelligence provides a practical framework for modelling the reasoning of economic agents in such situations. In strategic environments, agents can actually do better by behaving non-optimally. In such situations, it is thus in agents' strategic interests to make 'mistakes'. The actual method of reasoning used to solve the agents' problems can then be used as a form of precommitment, to influence the eventual outcomes.

This paper has sought to define the limits and possibilities for artificial intelligence in economic theory, rather than make a positive and substantive contribution and application as found in other papers in this volume. Whilst I do not see artificial intelligence as a new paradigm that will necessarily replace and supplant the orthodox economic model of rationality, it clearly has a great potential role, and one that will clearly become very important in future years.

9. Church's Thesis and Game Theory: An Overview of Some Results

Luca Anderlini

Introduction

It is hard to even imagine what economics would be like without the idea of 'rational agents'. As economic theory has developed in the last 30-40 years, the rational agents which populate the models have been asked to solve increasingly complex problems. Especially with the widespread use of game theory throughout the different fields of economics, our rational agents have been asked to perform tasks which in, some cases at least, are obviously unrealistically complex. Moreover, it has become a sort of conventional wisdom to ascribe to the 'over-rationality' of the players some of the unpalatable results which game theory sometimes generates.

This paper is not concerned with questions of realism as far as the computational ability of the players is concerned. Rather, it offers a brief overview of one strand of the literature on 'bounded rationality' which was initiated by Ken Binmore (1987) with a very influential paper. The basic stance behind this research agenda is very simple to outline. There exists a well-defined notion of 'computability', widely accepted by mathematicians. The widest possible intuitive notion of computability corresponds to a well-defined class of functions (general recursive functions), which in turn corresponds to the set of functions which can be computed by one of many equivalent classes of finite computing devices (or algorithms, or programs). The best known among such equivalent classes is probably the class of Turing machines. This view, known as Church's Thesis, is not without its very distinguished critics.[1] In its strongest form it goes as far as identifying what mathematical logic 'can or cannot do' with what can be computed by a Turing machine. The literature which I will briefly

---

[1] Penrose (1989).

review here concerns itself with the theory of games when the players are assumed to be able to perform only those tasks which are 'computable within Church's thesis' - those tasks which can be performed by a Turing machine. It is not concerned with issues of realism in at least two, related, senses. Firstly, it does not, as some other literature indeed does,[2] attempt to model the actual inner workings of the decision-making unit (the human brain!) with any degree of realism. Secondly, while imposing the constraint that agents' tasks should be capable of being carried out by a finite device in a finite number of steps, it does not impose any a priori bound on the actual size of the device or on the number of steps taken. The intellectual experiment performed could be described as exploring the 'limit case' of bounded rationality in games.

It should be added immediately that this is not the main avenue which has been explored so far in the game theoretic literature on bounded rationality. The literature on 'finite automata' playing repeated games and its various spin-offs is far larger than the one briefly reviewed here. It has been extremely influential as well - certainly on my own general views of the problem of bounded rationality. The list of even just the very important contributions would be far too long; I shall simply mention the pioneering work of Aumann (1981), Neyman (1985) and Rubinstein (1986).

The purpose of this paper is to report very briefly on the literature described above in a non-technical manner. I shall use some notation and refer to some formal tools, however. This is simply because without a minimum of these ingredients it is difficult to do justice to even the flavour of the results which I shall mention. Most of the assertions I will explicitly make are stated and demonstrated rigorously in the references I cite. Needless to say, I think anyone wanting to understand fully what is going on should go back to the original references.

The outline of the paper is as follows. In the next section I briefly set up some notation and discuss further the level of generality of the framework used later. In Section 3, I discuss one set of results

---

[2]   See, for instance, the chapter by Marris on 'neural nets' (this volume).

generated by the application of computability constraints to the analysis of some issues concerning the foundations of game theory. One could call the results discussed in this section 'impossibility results'. Section 4 gives an account of how the computability framework may help analyse games with a costless pre-play communication stage (cheap talk). The main results discussed here say that the computability framework is useful in constructing models in which pre-play communication matters as an equilibrium selection mechanism. Section 5 reports on some results concerning repeated games. Again, the computability framework is shown to be useful in the difficult task of selecting equilibrium payoffs within the large set supported by the 'folk theorem' of repeated games. Section 6 briefly concludes the paper.

Gödel Numbers

Turing machines are usually taken to compute functions from the natural numbers (*N*) into the natural numbers. It is not difficult, however, to extend the notion of computability to virtually any 'discrete' domain. This is done by means of a coding operation which assigns to any string of symbols drawn from a given finite alphabet a natural number. There are many alternative ways to perform such an operation, often referred to as the assignment of Gödel numbers. The intuition behind the feasibility of the coding is simple if one thinks of it in the following terms. First of all assign an 'alphabetical order' to the symbols in the fixed alphabet to be used. Imagine then to order in alphabetical order all the possible strings (or 'words') of length 2, then those of length 3, and so on up to any arbitrarily long strings. Each string is now coded by the number of its place in such (alphabetically ordered) list of strings. The coding operation just described not only is feasible but is obviously itself computable within Church's thesis. It follows that the domain and range of a computable function can always be taken to be *N* without any loss of generality.

Each Turing machine is identified by its 'program', which consists of a finite string of symbols obeying some syntactical rules. It follows that a second consequence of the feasibility of the coding operation described above is that the Turing machines themselves may be all assigned codes in N.[3] Throughout the rest of the paper the notation $\{X\}(Y)$ where X and Y are both natural numbers will stand for the result (if defined) of the computation carried out by Turing machine (with Gödel number) X when given as input the string (with Gödel number) Y. It should be noticed that the notation $\{X\}(Y)$ although strange at first sight, is perfectly admissible in this context. Like any other 'program', Turing machines may not *halt* (produce an output) on some or all inputs. The fact that the computation $\{X\}(Y)$ halts will be denoted by $\{X\}(Y)\downarrow$; the fact that it does not will be denoted by $\{X\}(Y)\uparrow$.

Impossibility Results

Take a one-shot two-player finite-action normal-form game, G, where neither player has a dominant strategy. In other words, what is best for player 1 does depend on player 2's choice and vice versa. The game G is also, for simplicity, assumed to have at least one Nash equilibrium in pure strategies. We now imagine the players to be two Turing machines. Each machine is given as input its own Gödel number, the Gödel number of the opposing player and the full description of the game.[4] The output of the Turing machines given such inputs is then taken to represent the actions of the players in the game G.

Given that a Nash equilibrium of the game G involves each player picking a strategy which is optimal given the choice of the other

---

[3]   This immediately proves that there are functions which cannot be computed by a Turing machine since there are at most N such functions but there are 2^{N_0} functions from N into N.

[4]   Not all one-shot two-player normal-form games can be coded into a natural number, but very mild restrictions will indeed make the coding possible. Canning (1988) discusses this at some length, one simple assumption which will do the job is that all payoffs are *rational* numbers.

player, the following question seems a natural one to ask about the set-up I have just described. For a fixed G, can we find a Turing machine, say, X, which will for *all* possible opposing players, say Y, play an action which is optimal given the action of Y? The answer is no. The first to ask the question and to find the answer was Ken Binmore (1987) in the paper which opened up the area which I am reviewing here. Anderlini (1990) partly reformulates the question and states and proves again that the answer is negative. The intuition behind the result is very simple to explain.

A standard result from the mathematical literature guarantees the existence of a 'universal Turing machine', say U, with the following characteristics. Given the Gödel number of any Turing machine, say M, and of any input string, say e, U *simulates* the computation $\{M\}(e)$ and, provided that $\{M\}(e)\downarrow$, gives the same result. (In terms of actual computer programs U can easily be thought of as a 'universal compiler'.) Consider now a machine Y in the set-up described above which performs the following operations. First simulate the computation of the opposing player $\{X\}(X;Y;G)$, and once the result of this computation has been established, Y is programmed to pick an action which makes the action chosen by the opposing player not optimal in G. It is now obvious that against such Y, machine X cannot possibly pick an optimal action in G. Machines like Y are sometimes referred to as 'diagonalizing' machines.

From the construction of Y it is not hard to see that this machine is making X necessarily wrong, but in a way which is in some sense costly. It is clear how in general Y will itself fail to pick an action which is optimal in G against the action chosen by X. The fact that such 'diagonalizing' machines are not 'optimal' in the sense above makes the following question a natural one to ask in the framework which I have just described.

Consider the set of machines which are rational in the following sense. Provided that the computation of the opposing player halts, the computation of a rational machine halts and prescribes an action which is optimal in G against the opponent's move.[5] (I will refer to such a set of machines as the 'set of rational players'.) Suppose now that we restrict attention to such machines only for both players. Can one get away from the impossibility result which I described above? In other words can one find a rational player, say X, which will halt (and hence play correctly) when faced with all possible rational players? The answer is again, and a little more surprisingly, negative. The result is stated and proved in Anderlini (1990). For any rational player, X, there exists another player Y, *also rational*, such that both $\{X\}(X;Y;G)\!\uparrow$ and $\{Y\}(X;Y;G)\!\uparrow$.

The intuition behind the result is not very hard to explain. Suppose that the set of rational players were 'well-behaved' enough so that there existed a Turing machine which could always answer correctly 'yes' or 'no' to the question 'is this player a member of the set of rational players?' when given as an input the Gödel number of such a player. Then the result I have just described could not possibly be true. For one could then construct a machine X as follows. X plays an arbitrarily chosen Nash equilibrium of G when Y is a rational player. When Y is not a rational player, X first simulates Y's computation and, if this computation halts, X outputs an action which is optimal in G against the action taken by Y. Clearly, such X would have precisely the characteristics which the result asserts are not possible. It follows that the set of rational players is *not* well behaved in the above sense.

This is indeed, in my view, the main insight to be gained from the exercise I have described.[6] It is not possible always to ascertain algorithmically whether an algorithm is rational or not in the above sense, even given a 'full description' of the algorithm in the form of its Gödel number. First-level knowledge of rationality seems to be

---

[5]   Notice that from the previous result it immediately follows that if a machine is rational in the sense just specified it will not always give an output (*halt*), for otherwise we would have found a machine with the precise characteristics which the previous result asserts are not possible.

[6]   McAfee (1984) made a very similar point in a single-person decision-theoretic context quite early on.

in trouble as a result of the computability constraints imposed on the players' abilities. The standard common knowledge of rationality assumption which is usual in game theory seems even more implausible as a result.

Pre-Play Communication

Consider a two-player one-shot game in strategic form *G*, where a coordination problem of the following sort is present.[7] Each player (i=1;2) has the choice of either strategy A_i or strategy B_i. If both players choose strategy A_i then they both get a payoff of 3. If they both opt for B_i, they both receive a payoff of 2. If one player chooses A_i and the other B_j (i=1;2 and i≠j), then both players obtain a payoff of 0. Evidently, both strategy pairs $(A_1;A_2)$ and $(B_1;B_2)$ constitute a Nash equilibrium of *G*. Both equilibria survive just about any refinement of the Nash equilibrium concept put forward in the literature (with the notable exception of Farrel 1983, 1988). The two equilibria are Pareto-rankable, however. There is a fairly wide consensus on the fact that there is 'something wrong' with the inefficient equilibrium $(B_1;B_2)$.

The informal argument one often hears against the inefficient equilibrium $(B_1;B_2)$ runs roughly as follows. The two players are rational and they both know that the other player is rational, and they know that the other player knows, ad infinitum. Rationality is common knowledge as well as the game *G* itself. Hence they both know that $(A_1;A_2)$ is a self-enforcing arrangement (a Nash equilibrium) just as much as $(B_1;B_2)$. Hence if it were ever to be the case that $(B_1;B_2)$ was going to be played, the players could 'talk themselves out of it'. They could talk each other into agreeing that

---

[7]   Throughout this and the next section I will refer to what is known as 'pure coordination' games (Schelling, 1963). All the results apply to a wider class of games, however. This is the class of 'common interest' games. A game is a common interest game if there is one pair of payoffs (which may be obtained by means of more than one pair of strategies) which *strictly* Pareto-dominates all other payoff pairs in the game.

since $(A_1;A_2)$ is a self-enforcing arrangement and it makes them *both* better off than $(B_1;B_2)$ they should both switch to the better equilibrium.

It is well known that the above argument is difficult to formalize. Indeed, in the standard game theoretic framework, the possibility of 'cheap talk' or 'pre-play communication' simply does not affect the set of payoffs which can be sustained in equilibrium. If communication is costless (it does not *directly* affect the pay-offs of the game to be played), then there is always a 'babbling' (subgame perfect) equilibrium in which players talk, maybe for a long time, maybe exchanging complex messages, and then proceed to ignore anything that has been said and play the inefficient equilibrium $(B_1;B_2)$. This is an obviously unsatisfactory state of affairs which the computability framework is able to rectify to a large extent.

Anderlini (1990) proposes the following solution to the problem. Consider a pair of Turing machines, X_1 and X_2, representing player 1 and 2's strategies in a game with pre-play communication as follows. First X_i (i = 1;2) is asked to produce a communication string, C_i. This is taken to be the output of X_i on a fixed arbitrary symbol, say ●, so that we take it to be the case that $\{X_i\}(●) = C_i$. Subsequently, the message strings are exchanged and the output of X_i on the pair of messages $(C_1;C_2)$ is taken to be the action of player *i* in *G*. In this way a larger normal-form game, Γ, is obtained where the strategy spaces on the side of each player are Turing machines.[8] Consider now the 'trembling-hand perfect' equilibria of this larger

---

[8]   McAfee (1984) and Howard (1988) analyse a model which differs from the one I have just outlined in three respects. Firstly, the game *G* to be played is a version of the prisoners' dilemma. Secondly, players are required to output as messages their true Gödel numbers. Thirdly, the equilibrium concept they use is that of evolutionarily stable strategies. They both find that, under the assumptions they make, cooperation can be enforced in the one-shot prisoners' dilemma.

game[9] which satisfy the requirements of: a) assigning strictly positive probability to a 'sufficiently large' set of strategies and b) the probability distributions of the mistakes of both players are themselves computable in an appropriate sense.[10] The main theorem in Anderlini (1990) guarantees that the only payoffs which can be obtained in such equilibria are the Pareto-efficient ones yielded by the pair of actions $(A_1;A_2)$.

Once more, the intuition behind the result which I have just described is not hard to outline. Relying on the existence of a universal Turing machine described in Section 3 and on a 'fixed point' result in the space of computable functions known in the mathematical literature as the 'recursion theorem' (cf. for instance Cutland, 1980), one can prove that the following is true. Given any admissible probability distribution, there exists a machine, say X_i, with the following characteristics. Firstly, X_i has strictly positive probability according to such admissible probability distribution. Secondly, the message, C_{Xi}, which X_i outputs, is such that the probability updated using Bayes' rule that the machine's action in the action-choosing stage of the game is B_i is arbitrarily close to zero. Thirdly, in the action-choosing stage of the game, machine X_i always (whatever the message of the opponent) plays action A_i. This is essentially what in Anderlini (1990) is called the 'communication lemma'. It states that in the above framework it is possible to find machines which will effectively communicate to the other player their intention to play cooperatively in the action-choosing stage of the

---

9   A trembling-hand perfect equilibrium is a 'perturbed' Nash equilibrium in which players make small 'mistakes' (these can also be interpreted as beliefs of the opposing player). In this context, the equilibrium strategy of each player is required to be optimal against a probability distribution over the strategies of the opposing player which assigns very high probability to the equilibrium strategy of the opposing player and a small amount to a large set of alternative strategies which the opposing player may play 'by mistake'.

10   Below, I refer to any probability distribution satisfying a) and b) above as an *admissible* probability distribution.

game.

The main result now follows relatively easily. The first thing to notice is that in any trembling-hand equilibrium of the larger game Γ, one must have the equilibrium machines for both players using correctly Bayes' rule, in the sense of playing an action in G which is optimal given the probability distribution obtained updating the 'tremble' of the opposing player on the basis of the messages observed. This is simply a consequence of the fact that equilibrium machines are required to be optimal in expected terms given the tremble of the opposing player. Suppose that we had a trembling-hand perfect equilibrium of Γ (with admissible trembles) in which payoffs for both players are strictly below 3. Consider now a machine for player 1, like X_i described above. Since the equilibrium machine for player 2, say X^*_2, is a correct Bayesian optimizer, by the communication lemma, when X^*_2 observes message C_{X1}, it must respond by playing action A_2 in G. Hence machines X_1 and X^*_2 playing against each other both obtain a payoff of 3. Since machine X^*_2 has probability very close to one in player 2's tremble, it now follows that the *expected* payoff of machine X_1 against player 2's tremble is arbitrarily close to 3. The equilibrium machine for player 1 also has to be optimal against the tremble of player 2 in expected terms. Hence it must do at least as well as X_1. Hence the expected payoff to X^*_1 is also arbitrarily close to 3. A symmetric argument can be used to show that the expected payoff to X^*_2 is also arbitrarily close to 3, hence establishing the result.

Repeated Games

When a given stage game is repeated infinitely many times, a staggering multiplicity of equilibria emerges as players discount the future less and less (or not at all). The 'Folk theorem' of repeated games states that in the limit, any vector of long-run payoffs which is 'individually rational' can be sustained as an equilibrium. Thus, although 'cooperation' can be sustained as an equilibrium, it is not the only possible outcome. The result is true regardless of how appealing the cooperative outcome may be relative to others, given the 'structure' of the stage game. Consider in particular the infinite repetition of the stage game G, described in the previous section. Intuitively, non-efficient outcomes result from a lack of coordination. If players interact for a long time, it should be possible for each player to take actions early in the repeated game to signal and convince others that he will play the efficient action A_i in the future, and as a result the efficient pay-off (3;3) will evolve if players discount the future at a sufficiently small rate. The results in Anderlini and Sabourian (1991) formalize the above intuition. To be more precise, if the game is sufficiently perturbed (i.e. if players make mistakes or if the players are not fully convinced of the identity of others) and if players choose strategies which can be implemented by Turing machines, then, for the case of little or no discounting, the equilibrium payoffs shrink to the efficient pair as the perturbation becomes negligible.[11]

The main line of argument behind the result I have just described is very close to the intuitive reasoning of the previous section. (The technical details are considerably more complex, however.) The analogue of the communication lemma in this context states that one can find 'revealing' machines which will use their actions in the early stages of the game to reveal their intention to switch to the cooperative action from a certain date onwards. The rest of the reasoning is again analogous to the one described earlier. Exploiting the structure of the stage game G, one can show that the revelation of the intention to play the cooperative action from a certain date onwards is sufficient to destroy any equilibrium of the repeated game not yielding (approximately) an average payoff of 3 to both players.

---

[11]   Aumann and Sorin (1989) prove a result which is very similar to Anderlini and Sabourian (1991). The hypotheses on which the two results rest are quite different, however. In Aumann and Sorin the equilibrium strategies of the players are not restricted to be computable. The rest of the strategies which are given positive probability by the players' trembles are restricted to be of bounded memory and to be 'reactive' in the sense that the action of a player at time t is taken to be a function of the other player's action up to t-1 rather than of the whole history (including a player' *own* actions) of the game up to t-1.

Concluding Remarks

A model which is widely accepted and extensively studied in mathematics exists which lends itself to the study of the limit case of bounded rationality in game theory. I have done no more than briefly report some of the results which this computability framework has yielded so far in the study of strategic interactions. This is a small, unfortunately very technical, literature not accessible to many. Hopefully, I will have enticed at least some to go back to the original references for further reading.

10. The Development of Intelligent Macroeconometric Models and Modelling Procedures

Mike Artis, Scott Moss and Paul Ormerod

Introduction

Many refinements and advances have been made to macroeconomic models over the past fifteen years. These cover both the economic content of the models and the econometric techniques which are used to estimate them. In terms of forecasting accuracy, however, it is by no means clear that the 1980s have seen improvements on what was achieved in the mid to late 1970s.

It is the lack of improvement in forecasting accuracy during the past decade which motivates our view that the traditional econometric-based approach needs to be augmented with expert systems technology if further progress is to be made.

A number of detailed studies both in the UK and the US have shown that the adjustment of the output of a macro-model by an experienced model operator usually leads to an improvement in the accuracy of forecast compared to the pure output of the model. Turner (1990) is perhaps the most recent contribution to this literature. This suggests that forecasters possess knowledge about how the economy operates which is additional to the information contained in the mathematical equations which make up the mode. (Part of this knowledge will simply be information about the current state of the economy (e.g. the precise level at which a key wage settlement has been made), but there is also knowledge about the structural relations of the economy which the model operator uses to shape the forecast output.)

Advances in artificial intelligence technology in recent years makes it feasible to consider developing a system which augments the econometric relationships of a macroeconomic model with the knowledge of experienced model operators. The potential advantage of this is three-fold. First, the codifying of existing practices in an expert system will enable the scarce resource of the operator's time to be saved, leaving him or her to concentrate on questions of particular difficulty. In other words, the expert system can operate as a productivity-enhancing tool. Second, codifying the expertise of an operator or team of operators means that this knowledge is not lost to the organization when members of the team leave for whatever reason. Organizations make investments in skilled individuals, and expert systems enable the value of that investment to be retained even if an individual leaves. The third point is more ambitious, and is that codifying the knowledge of experienced forecasters - particularly if this is done is a way which permits learning to take place subsequently - might increase our understanding of how the economy actually operates.

The feasibility of using expert systems to build single-equation econometric models has already been demonstrated. Ormerod (1985-87) has led a team which successfully developed an expert system for the building of single-equation econometric models which is now in commercial use by companies such as Proctor and Gamble, Mars and British Telecom. Moss (1989a, 1989b) has conducted simulation experiments with microeconomic models demonstrating that the properties of machine-learning techniques using set theory and logic are of practical value.

Further development of AI techniques in the context of macroeconometric modelling seems promising for two reasons. First, the complexities of both models and the environment relative to current information technology make macroeconomics a natural target for the application of artificial-intelligence techniques. Advances in information technology over the past twenty years have not reduced palpably the complexity of the environment relative to our abilities to model it: but they have made possible developments in artificial intelligence which enable researchers to cope better with that complexity.

The second reason is that the econometric techniques developed for modelling macro-data sets in the 1970s and 1980s have been very thoroughly exploited. A further leap forward is needed to produce improvements in forecasting and, ultimately, policy analysis. Whilst the refinement of existing econometric methodologies to grapple with the problem of structural change is one important and relevant response, more than likely the adoption of new methodologies is called for. Ormerod (1990a, 1990b) has reported results with neural network technology which out-perform published single-equation econometric models. In this paper, we concentrate on the potential of expert systems to augment existing macroeconomic models.

The Case for a New Approach to Macro-Modelling

Macroeconometric modelling became strikingly more sophisticated from the mid 1970s through to the early 1980s. First, new approaches to estimation were exploited, following the demonstration by Hendry and his colleagues (Davidson et al (1978); Hendry and Mizon (1978b), of the power of the error correction approach. This reformulation of accepted procedures proved very useful in capturing dynamics, both on its own and as the second stage of the two-step cointegration/error correction procedure of Engle and Granger (1987). Second, the scope of macro-model specification was extended by grafting a financial sector onto an elaborated IS curve, and subsequently by attempts to model 'the supply side'. Third, model solution techniques have been extended to include routine consistent expectations solutions.

These substantial achievements in technique have nevertheless to be set beside the lack of general improvement in forecast accuracy since the late 1970s. Burns (1986) did find that the longer term (two year ahead) UK Treasury forecasts, adjusted for changes in the inherent noisiness of the environment, had improved in the early 1980s compared to the 1970s, but he could find no such improvement in the short-term forecasts. McNees (1988) was able to come to a more optimistic conclusion for US forecasts, but Wallis (1989), who extended the methodology of Burns to other UK forecasts, could report no clear instances of improvement. More recently, although no systematic study exists as yet, it is clear that in the UK, forecasters failed almost completely to anticipate the size of the current account deficit which has emerged in the past two years, and were far too optimistic in general about economic prospects for 1990.

The Contribution of an AI Approach

Expert Systems and Forecasting

An expert system codifies the practices of experts in reaching decisions and forming judgements. A macro-model can be viewed as a half-formed approach to an expert system in this sense: it formally embodies numerical rules based on statistical estimation and identities without embodying (usually) expert judgements arrived at by other means. Yet it is well documented that in forecasting applications, judgement is continually imposed on the model, generally through the adjustment of equation intercepts and inevitably through the assumptions of future values of exogenous variables.

Osborne and Teal (1979) found in their postmortem of forecasts conducted on the National Institute model that it is as if the forecasters have a 'latent model' implicit in their interventions. Interventions on the model appeared to counter 'extravagant' trajectories for exogenous variables. In a complementary study, Artis (1982) noted that residual adjustments across UK macroeconometric models tend to offset differences in the formal (ie. written down) models themselves. More recently, Wallis and Whitley (1990) found that errors in assumed future values of exogenous variables tended to reduce model error when compared with retrospective forecasts using the actual values of the exogenous variables. That is, the assumed values tend to be wrong in directions which improve the forecast values of the main endogenous variables. Moreover, adjustments to intercepts or other coefficients of the models are used to force models to generate values conforming to the prior views of the forecasters. 'If this were applied to large numbers of variables, one could conclude that the role of the model in producing the forecast was relatively minor.' Indeed, in one case the 'published forecast was largely imposed on the model'.

Turner (1990) in a detailed analysis of the LBS and NIESR forecasts in the UK, concludes that 'the forecasters' judgement does indeed exert a strong influence on the forecasts of the main macro-variables. Furthermore, in a number of the cases examined it is apparent that the forecasters' intuitive judgement is at least as important as any formal off-model calculation'.

The Artificially Intelligent Macroeconomic Forecasting System: Overall Design

The current position in relation to macroeconometric forecasting is indicated in Figure 1. Both the system of equations and the forecasters provide information to the forecasting system. The system reports the results, the model managers note anomalies and implausible endogenous variable values, adjust equation intercepts in order to correct the results and, with the new intercepts, the system of revised equations is used to generate a revised forecast. The four-step iteration indicated by the loop in the lower right of Figure 1 continues until the forecasters are satisfied with the result.

It is not difficult to see that a starting version, at least, of 'the complete model' might be better described as the existing formal version together with the rules for its use in forecasting applications. Expert-systems application could claim to deliver such a complete model. We note three qualifications and three extensions.

The qualifications are, first, that the expert-system element might not be completely general, i.e. usable for any model. More likely, there would be one expert system suitable for model A, another for model B, and so on. Second, one function of the model intervention is to incorporate extra-model information which is ephemeral - e.g. news about a strike or a record-keeping failure which affects the economy in a particular way at a particular time. No reasonable general rule can replace this; but a well-designed system would accommodate the appropriate intervention and clarify the results. Third, it cannot be guaranteed that the rulebase will not contain its own misspecifications. In a fully developed version, however, we believe that the model can be made self-improving by application of machine-based learning procedures.

The extensions are, first, that an expert systems approach permits the model base to be composed of a mixed set of numerical rules, both estimated and imposed, and conditional logic rules.

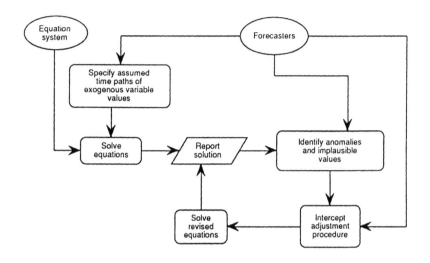

Figure 10.1 *Flowchart of macroeconomic forecasting process*

Incorporation of the latter would allow for the judgements of the forecasters to be incorporated formally and consistently in their published forecasts. Even if we accept that the need for such judgements implies an underlying misspecification of the numerical rules, those rules still impose an underlying consistency on the expert-system-augmented model. Second, the expert system can be written to incorporate machine-based learning. Such an extension goes beyond expert-system applications which codify sets of rules based on existing knowledge. The extension would involve, for example, automated post-mortem examinations and repeated in-run evaluations of the usefulness of additional inputs to time-series forecasts. Third, an appropriately specified expert-system module would provide explanations of the reasons for assumed values of exogenous variables and for any intercept or other residual adjustment. Such explanations would be part of the forecast output.

In the simplest version of an artificially intelligent forecasting system, the direct role of the forecasters is replaced by four sets of rules. One set formulates assumptions about the future values of exogenous variables. A second set decides the residual adjustment. A third identifies anomalies and the fourth corrects them. The new role of the forecasters is to oversee and, when they wish, to override the application of the rules.

In this set-up, an expert system does not attempt to capture every single piece of knowledge which exists, and does not remove entirely the role of human expertise. But human experts using such a system are able to devote their time to particularly difficult questions which arise in the construction of a forecast. It should be said that any modifications which the operators make should be noted, with a view to assessing whether the system could be improved by the subsequent incorporation of this knowledge.

A summary flow chart for the system is given in Figure 2. In this forecasting system, the forecasters manage the development of the forecast. The rulebases provide for the 'routine' residual adjustments of the model. The forecasters can supplement the rule-determined adjustments - a role which is natural and important when significant but ephemeral events occur which the model cannot take endogenously into account. We thus have a slightly more elaborate iterative loop in the lower right of Figure 2 than in Figure 1. The iterations can stop either because some stopping rule from the rulebase is satisfied or because the forecasters do not wish to proceed further.

Explanation Facilities

An important part of a forecaster's role should be to explain the structure and content of any given forecast. Different organizations devote different amounts of resources to disseminating such explanations, both internally and externally.

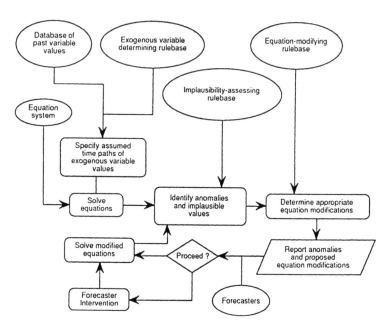

Figure 10.2 *Flowchart of an artificially intelligent macroeconomic forecasting system*

Full explanation facilities are essential. This is because, in the proposed system, the forecaster's principal role is that of a manager of the system. In the first place, successful management requires access to information about what is being done and the reasons for doing it. If the reasons seem unsatisfactory, then it must be open to the forecaster to add new rules or change existing rules. Second, the explanations can form part of the published forecasts, thereby to enable users to assess the validity of the forecasts for their particular purposes. The third reason relates to evaluations of the forecasting system. Forecasting accuracy can be assessed objectively, as it is presently. However, the plausibility of the way the model works, how intercepts are adjusted and the quality of any policy analyses derived for the forecasting system must depend on an appeal to informed intuition. In order to inform the intuition, the model must generate detailed explanations of its actions and conclusions.

In most expert systems, explanations are given in response to 'why' questions (e.g. 'Why did the system sell all 9 per cent 1992 gilts?') or in response to 'how' questions (e.g. 'How were the 9 per cent 1992 gilts sold?'). In response to the 'why' questions, the system will list the conditions which triggered the gilt-selling rule. In response to the 'how' questions, the system will list the actions indicated by the rule. This information is useful, but insufficient for our purposes.

A different (and for our purposes preferable) means of providing explanations in expert systems was proposed by Cohen (1985). He suggested that data and rules could be given endorsements. For example, a rule which has worked well repeatedly could be endorsed as 'reliable', or as 'important-when-true'. Data could similarly be endorsed as 'reliable' or 'unreliable' or perhaps 'from-normally-reliable-sources-. Rules would then be triggered at least in part on the basis of their endorsements. The advantage of this system is that the answer to a 'why' question would include the endorsements of the data which triggered a rule and the rule itself. The endorsements and the conditions in which they are attached to rules and data can themselves be determined from the experts whose knowledge informs the system.

System Self-Maintenance

It is desirable that the forecasting system should maintain itself. Such an extension of the system would be particularly challenging, but again it does not seem to be beyond the bounds of feasibility.

Rules which systematically yield good or improved forecasts can be endorsed as such, and so will tend to be used in preference to less well endorsed rules. Since these endorsements accumulate with experience, the system will in effect be evaluating its own performance and then acting on that evaluation. In addition, the system can endorse unsuccessful rules as such, delete them from their respective rulebases and replace them with some more promising variant. Moss has developed and used such a self-maintenance scheme in the context of microeconomic modelling.

An alternative to such schemes is based on genetic algorithms which stimulate biological evolution to solve problems involving optimization - including optimization of rulebases.   Genetic algorithms are superior to conventional optimizing techniques based on calculus or topology when environments are complex and relationships are non-linear. The best established genetic algorithms derive from the work by John Holland in the 1970s, as reported by, for example, Goldberg (1989). These algorithms are computationally efficient provided that they respond entirely to payoff information and not to any other knowledge which is specific to the problem at hand. In relation to macroeconomic forecasting, payoff would be some numerical measure of goodness of resulting forecasts. Customary concerns with these algorithms pertain to the quality of the result and to computational efficiency based in practice on the use of analogies drawn from the theory of biological evolution. However, there is no scope for the application of an endorsement scheme to such algorithms or, therefore, the extensive explanations facility we require which we suggest must be part of an AI application to macro forecasting.

Conclusion

Despite refinements and advances, both in the economic content of macro-models and in the econometric techniques used to construct them, little progress has been made during the past decade in terms of forecasting accuracy.

It is the lack of improvement in forecasting accuracy during the past decade which motivates our view that the traditional econometric-based approach needs to be augmented with expert-systems technology if further progress is to be made.

Advances in artificial-intelligence technology in recent years make it feasible to consider developing a system which augments the econometric relationships of a macro-economic model with the knowledge of experienced model operators.

Bibliography

Abreu, D., Rubenstein, A. (1988), 'The Structure of Nash-Equilibria in Repeated Games with Finite Automata', *Econometrica*, (56), 1259-1281.

Akerlof, G. and Yellen, J. (1985), 'A Near Rational Model of the Business Cycle with Wage and Price Inertia', *Quarterly Journal of Economics*, (100), 823-838.

Altman, J. (1989), 'Deceptively Simple Behaviour', *Nature*, No. 6429.

Anderlini, L. (1990), 'Some Notes on Church's Thesis and the Theory of Games', *Theory and Decision*, 29: 19-52.

Anderlini, L. and Sabourian, H. (1991), *Cooperation and Effective Computability*, Cambridge University, mimeo.

Arifovic, J. (1990), *Learning by Genetic Algorithms in Economic Environments*, Santa Fe Institute Working Paper 90-001.

Arrow, K. (1962), 'The Economics of Scanning by Doing', *Review of Economic Studies*, pp.155-73.

Arthur, W.B. (1990), 'The Program's Research' in *Emergent Structures*, Santa Fe Institute.

Artis, M.J. (1982), *Why Do Forecasts Differ?*, paper presented to the Academic Panel, Bank of England.

Aumann, R.J. (1981), 'Survey of Repeated Games', in *Essays in Game Theory and Mathematical Economics in Honor of Oskar Morgenstern*, Mannheim: Bibliographisches Institut, 11-42.

Aumann, R.J. and Sorin, S. (1989), 'Cooperation and Bounded

Recall', *Games and Economic Behavior*, 1:5-39.

Axelrod, R. (1984), *The Evolution of Cooperation*, London: Penguin.
Baars, B. (1988), A Cognitive Theory of Consciousness, Cambridge:
Cambridge University Press.

Baddeley, A. (1986), *Working Memory*, Oxford: Oxford University
Press.

Bentham, J. (1789), 'Introduction to the Principles of Morals and
Legislation', in Warnock, 3:179-214.M (ed.), *Utilitarianism*,
Fontana.

Bentley, J. and Saxe, J. (1980), 'An Analysis of Two Heuristics for
the Euclidean Travelling Salesman Problem', *Proceedings of 18th
Allerton Conference of Communication, Control and Computing*.

Binmore, K. (1987), 'Modeling Rational Players', *Economics and
Philosophy*.

Brander, J. and Spencer, B. (1983), 'Strategic Commitment with
R&D: The Symmetric Case', *Bell Journal*, (14), 225-35.

Burns, T. (1986), *The Interpretation and Use of Economic
Predictions*, Proceedings of the Royal Society, Series A, pp.103-25.

Canning, D. (1988), 'Rationality and Game Theory When Players
are Turing Machines', *S.T.I.C.E.R.D. Discussion Paper 88/183*,
London School of Economics, London.

Charniack, E. and McDermott, D. (1985), *Introduction to Artificial
Intelligence*, Reading, Massachusetts: Addison-Wesley.

Charniack, E., Rierbeck, C., McDermott, D. and Meehan, F.
(1987), *Artifical Intelligence Programming*, Hillindale, New Jersey:
Sawrente Erlbaum Associates.

Cohen, P.R. (1985), *Heuristic Reasoning Under Uncertainty: An Artificial Intelligence Approach*, London: Pitman.

Coombs, R., Saviotti, P. and Walsh, V. (1987), *Economics and Technological Change*, Hampshire: Macmillan.

Crick, F. and Kock, C. (1990), 'Towards a Neurobiological Theory of Consciousness', *Seminars in the Neurosciences*, pp.66-72.

Cutland, N.J. (1980), *Computability*, Cambridge: Cambridge University Press.

Cyert, R.M. and March, J.G. (1963), *A Behavioural Theory of the Firm, Englewood Cliffs*, NJ: Prentice Hall.

Damasio, A. (1989), 'The Brain Binds Entities and Events by Multiregional Activation from Convergence Zones', *Journal of Neural Computation*, pp176-192.

Dasgupta, P. (1986), 'The Theory of Technological Competition', in K Binmore and P Dasgupta (eds), *Economic Organization as Games*, Oxford: Blackwell, pp.139-164.

Davidson, J.E.H., Hendry, D.F., Sbra, F., and Yeo, S. (1978), 'Econometric Modelling of the Aggregate Time Series Relationship Between Consumers' Expenditure and Income in the United Kingdom', *Economic Journal*, 88, December, pp. 661-92.

Davis, R. and Serat, D. (1982), *Knowledge-Based Systems in Artificial Intelligence*, New York: McGraw-Hill.

Dixon, H.D. (1987), 'Approximate Bertrand Equilibria in a Replicated Industry', *Review of Economic Studies*, (54), 47-62.

Dixon, H.D. (1988), 'Oligopoly Theory Made Simple', in Davies et al, *The Economics of Industrial Organization*, London: Longmans, pp.127-165.

Dixon, H.D. (1990), 'Equilibrium and Explanation', in Creedy, J.(ed.), *The Foundation of Economic Thought*, Oxford: Blackwells, pp356-93.

Egidi, M. and Marris, R. (eds) (1992), *Herbert Simon, Economics, Bounded Rationality and the Cognitive Revolution*, London: Edward Elgar.

Engle, R.F. and Granger, C.W.J. (1987), 'Dynamic Model Specification and Equilibrium Constraints: Cointegration and Error Correction', *Econometrica*, 55, pp. 251-76.

Ericsson, K. and Simon, H. A. (1984a), 'Verbal Reports as Data', *Psychological Review*, 87 (3).

Ericsson, K. and Simon H. A. (1984b), *Protocol Analysis*, MIT Press.

Farrel, J. (1983), *Meaning and Credibility in Cheap-Talk Games*, University of California at Berkeley, mimeo.

Farrel, J. (1988), 'Communication, Coordination and Nash Equilibrium', *Economics Letters*, 27:209-214.

Fisher, F.M. (1989), 'Games Economists Play: A Non-cooperative View', *Rand Journal of Economics*, 20 (10), Spring, pp. 113-124.

Forgy, C. and McDermott, J. (1976), *The OPS Reference Manual*, Department of Computer Science, Carnegie-Mellon University, Pittsburgh.

Friedman, M. (1953), *Essays in Positive Economics*, Chicago: University of Chicago Press.

Fudenberg, D., Gilbert, R., Stiglitz, J. and Tirole, J. (1983), 'Preemption, Leapfrogging and Competition in Patent Races', *European Economic Review*, 22, 3-31.

Gilad, B. and Kaish, S. (ed.), (1986), *Handbook of Behavioural Economics*, Vol A, London: JAI Press.

Goldberg, D.E. (1989), *Genetic Algorithms in Search, Optimization and Machine Learning*, Reading, MA: Addison-Wesley.

Hall, R. and Hitch, C. (1951), 'Price Theory and Business Behaviour' in *Oxford Studies in the Price Mechanism*, Andrews and Wilson (eds), Oxford: Oxford University Press.

Harmon, P. and King, D. (1985), *Expert Systems*, New York: Wiley Press.

Hart, O. (1979), 'Monopolistic Competition in a Large Economy with Differential Commodities', *Review of Economic Studies*, (46), 1-30.

Hebb, D. (1949), *The Organization of Behaviour*, New York: John Wiley.

Heiner, R. A. (1983), 'The Origin of Predictable Behaviour', *American Economic Review*, 73 (4), 560-595.

Hendry, D.F. (1988), 'Encompassing Implications of Feedback Versus Feedforward Mechanisms in Econometrics', *Oxford Economic Papers*, 40, pp.132-49.

Hendry, D.F. and Mizon Graham, E. (1978b), 'Serial Correlation as a Convenient Simplification, Not a Nuisance: A Comment on a Study of the Demand for Money by the Bank of England', *Economic Journal*, 88, pp. 549-563.

Hodges, A. (1983), *The Enigma of Intelligence*, London: Hutchinson.

Hogarth, M. with Reder M. (eds), (1986), *Rational Choice*, Chicago: University of Chicago Press.

Hogarth, R. (1980), *Judgement and Choice*, New York: Wiley.

Howard, J.V. (1988), 'Cooperation in the Prisoner's Dilemma', *Theory and Decision*, 24: 203-213.

Jackendorf, R. (1987), *Consciousness and the Computational Mind*, Cambridge, Mass.: MIT Press.

Johnson, G. and Scholes, K. (1989), *Exploring Corporate Strategy*, Englewood Cliffs, New Jersey: Prentice Hall.

Johnson-Laird, P. (1988), *The Computer and the Mind*, Cambridge, Mass.: Harvard Press.

Kahneman, D. and Tversky, A. (1979), 'Prospect Theory: An Analysis of Decision Under Risk', *Econometrica*, Vol 47, 263-291.

Kahneman, D. and Tverskey, A. (1984), 'Choices, Values and Frames', *Psychologist*, p. 1-10.

Kalai & Stanford, (1988), 'Finite Rationality and Interpersonal Complexity in Repeated Games', *Econometrica*, (56), 397-410.

Keynes, J. M. (1921), *A Treatise on Probability*, London: MacMillan.

Kilstrom, J. (1987), 'The Cognitive Unconscious', *Science*.

Knight, F. (1921), *Risk Uncertainty and Profit*, New York: Houghton Mifflan.

Koopmans, T.C. (1957), *Three Essays in the State of Economic Science*, New York: McGraw Hill.

Loomes, G. and Sugden, R. (1982), 'Regret Theory: An Alternative Theory of Rational Choice Under Uncertainty', *Economic Journal*, Vol 92, 805-824.

Mansfield, E. (1981), 'Imitation Costs and Patents: An Empirical Study', *Economic Journal*, 91, 907-18.

Marimon, R., McGrattan, E. and Sargent, T. (1989), 'Money as a Medium of Exchange in an Economy with Artificially Intelligent Agents', *Santa Fe Institute Working Paper 89-04*.

Marris, R. (1964), *Managerial Capitalism*, London: Macmillan.

Marshall, A. (1920), *Principles of Economics*, New York: Macmillan.

Masuch, M. and Warglein, M. (eds), (1991), *Artificial Intelligence in Organization and Management Theory*, Amsterdam: Elsevier.

McAfee, R.P. (1984), *Effective Computability in Economic Decisions*, University of Western Ontario, mimeo.

McNees, S. (1988), 'How Accurate are Macroeconomic Forecasts?', *New England Economic Review*, July/August, pp. 15-36.

Miller, G. (1956), 'The Magical Number Seven: Some Limits on our Capacity for Processing Information', *Psychological Review*, pp. 81-97.

Miller, J.H. (1989), 'The Coevolution of Automata in the Repeated Prisoner's Dilemma', *Working Paper 89-0003*, Santa Fe Institute.

Mintzberg, H. (1976), 'The Structure of Unstructured Decision Processes', *Administrative Science Quarterly*, p. 246-275.

Moravec, H. (1989), *Mind Children*, Cambridge, Mass.: Harvard University Press.

Moss, S.J. (1981), *An Economic Theory of Research Strategy*, Oxford: Basil Blackwell.

Moss, S.J. (1989a), *Control Metaphors in the Modelling of Decision-Making Behaviour*, University of Manchester Discussion Paper.

Moss, S.J. (1989b), *Firm Behaviour Out of Equilibrium: An Artificial Intelligence Approach*, University of Manchester Discussion Paper.

Nelson, R. and Winter, S. (1982), *An Evaluatory Theory of Economic Change*, Cambridge, Massachusetts: Harvard University Press.

Newell, A. and Simon, H. A. (1972), *Human Problem Solving*, Englewood Cliffs, New Jersey: Prentice Hall.

Neymen, A. (1985), 'Bounded Complexity Justifies Cooperation in the Finitely Repeated Prisoners' Dilemma', *Economic Letters*, 19:227-229.

Nisbett, R. and Wilson, T. (1977), 'Telling More Than We Know: Verbal Reports on Mental Processes', *Psychological Review*, Vol 84, pp. 231-259.

Ormerod, P. (1985-7), *Reports to the Emex-Alvey Club Consortium of the Department of Trade and Industry*, London.

Ormerod, P., Taylor, J. and Walker, A. (1990), 'Neural Networks in Economics' in Taylor, M. (ed.), *Developments in Monetary Analysis*, Oxford: Blackwells, pp.65-78.

Ormerod, P. and Walker, A. (1990), *Neural Networks and the Monetary Base in Switzerland*, Discussion Paper and IED project, Henley Centre, London.

Osborne, D.R. and Teal, F. (1979), 'An Assessment and Comparison of Two NIESR Econometric Model Forecasts', *National Institute Economic Review*, 88, pp. 50-62.

Penrose, E. (1959), *The Theory of the Growth of the Firm*.

Penrose, R. (1989), *The Emperor's New Mind*, Oxford: Oxford University Press.

Polya, G. (1957), *How to Solve It*, Princeton, NJ.: Princeton University Press.

Quandt, R. (1983), 'Computational Problems and Methods', *Handbook of Econometrics*, Vol 1, pp. 699-764.

Radner, R. (1966). 'Competitive Equilibrium Under Uncertainty', *Econometrica*, pp. 31-59.

Radner, R. (1980), *Journal of Economic Theory*.

Rae, J. (1987), *Behavioural Process Models: The Development of Principles and Practice in the Sphere of Economics*, DPhil Thesis, University of York.

Rae, J. and Reynolds, M. (1983), 'Information Processing and Economic Decision Making', *Business Studies Department Working Paper*, Sheffield City Polytechnic.

Rauch-Hindin, W.B. (1987), *A Guide to Commercial Artificial Intelligence*, New Jersey: Prentice Hall.

Reynolds, M.L. (1989), *Behavioural Models of Decision Making in Economics*, DPhil Thesis, University of York.

Robbins, L. (1935), *An Essay on the Nature and Significance of Economic Science*, London: MacMillan.

Rosenberg, M. (1982), 'The Economics of Using', in *Inside the Black Box*, Cambridge: Cambridge University Press.

Roth, A.E. (1991), 'Game Theory as Part of Empirical Economics', *Economic Journal*, 101, 404, 107-114.

Rubenstein, A. (1986), 'Finite Automata Play the Repeated Prisoner's Dilemma', *Journal of Economic Theory*, (3a), 83-96.

Rummelhart, D. and McClelland, L. (1988), *Explorations in Parallel Distributed Processing*, Cambridge, Mass.: MIT Press.

Schelling, T. C. (1963), *The Strategy of Conflict*, New York: Oxford University Press.

Serat, D. (1982), 'AM: Discovery in Mathematics as Heuristic Search' in Davis and Serat, *Knowledge-Based Systems in Artificial Intelligence*, New York: McGraw-Hill.

Simon, H.A. (1960), *The New Science of Management Decision*, New York: New York University Press.

Simon, H.A. (1976), 'From Substantive to Procedural Rationality' in Latsis, S. J. (ed.), *Method and Appraisal in Economics*, Cambridge: Cambridge University Press.

Simon, H.A. (1978), 'Rationality as Process and Product of Thought', *American Economic Review*, pp. 1-16.

Simon, H.A. (1978), *The Uses of Mathematics in the Social Sciences, Mathematics and Computers in Simulation*, Vol 20, 159-166.

Simon, H.A. (1979a), 'Rational Decision Making in Business Organizations', *American Economic Review*, Vol 69, 493-513.

Simon, H.A. (1979b), 'Information Processing Models of Cognition', *Annual Review of Psychology*, Vol 30, 363-396.

Simon, H.A. (1987), 'Decision Making and Problem Solving, *Interfaces*, pp. 11-31.

Sims, C.A. (1982), 'Policy Analyses with Econometric Models',

Brookings Papers in Economic Activity, 1, pp. 107-152.

Soasby, B. (1991), *Equilibrium and Evolution*, Manchester: Manchester University Press.

Solow, R.M. (1957), 'Technical Change and the Aggregate Production Function', *Review of Economics and Statistics*, 39, 312-20.

Tirole, J. (1989), *The Theory of Industrial Organization*, Cambridge, Mass.: MIT Press.

Turner, D.I. (1990), 'The Role of Judgement in Macroeconomic Forecasting', *Journal of Forecasting*, 9, (4), pp. 315-346.

Vickers, J. (1985), 'Delegation and the Theory of the Firm', *Economic Journal*, (95 Supplement), pp. 138-147.

Wallis, K.F. (1989), 'Macroeconomic Forecasting: A Survey', *Economic Journal*, 99, March, pp. 28-61.

Wallis, K.F. and Whitley, J.D. (1990), *Sources of Error in Forecasts and Expectations: UK Economic Models*, 1984-88, University of Warwick: ESRC Macroeconomic Modelling Bureau.

Warglein, M. (1991), 'Exit, Voice and Learning' in Masuch and Warglein (1991).

Waterman, D. and Hayes-Roth, F. (eds), (1978), *Pattern Directed Inference Systems*, New York: Academic Press.

Winston, P.H. and Horn, B.K.P. (1981), *LISP*, Reading, Mass: Addison-Wesley.

Index

Printed and bound by CPI Group (UK) Ltd, Croydon, CR0 4YY

28/10/2024

14581344-0001